Gunfighting, and Other Thoughts about Doing Violence

Volume Two

Version 1.1

To The Reader

PART ONE: MIND, BODY, SPIRIT

PART TWO: WAYS, MEANS, MANNERS

To The Reader

The content of this book confines itself almost completely to contemplation of lethal-force attacks, attacks meant to kill, maim, or cause grave injury or harm. This book does not consider anything other than lethal-force attacks that require lethal-force responses. This should not be taken as advice to the reader about responses to less than lethal-force felony assault. Neither should this report be taken as legal or technical guidance to you, the reader. This content of this book is intended for information and consideration, to provoke thought and discussion, and to encourage those who read it to seek professional advice and instruction. That is the primary and central intent of this book. The reader is strongly advised to consult with local authorities and those knowledgeable of the laws regarding and restricting use of force at all levels in their area, and to educate themselves so that they can, ahead of time, know how best to respond to assault. Don't wait to be attacked to think about what the law says you can or can't do, and don't wait until you're attacked to develop the skills you need to survive the attack. Do your homework now, do your thinking about legal response and force levels before and not during the attack, and get the training that will help you avoid an attack or survive one sooner rather than later.

No one involved in the production or publication of this book assumes responsibility or liability for any accident or injury that readers may put upon themselves by use, misuse and/or misinterpretation of this material. **This book is not a substitute for guidance and training by a professional instructor or expert. What you do with the information and opinions contained herein and the results of your actions is <u>your</u> responsibility and <u>only</u> yours.**

By continuing on with the reading of this book, you acknowledge that you have read, understand, and accept full responsibility for any and all use, misuse, interpretation, misinterpretation, understanding or misunderstanding of anything you see here or in supporting media, and agree that all parties involved with production, publication, and distribution of this book and supporting media and materials will not be held responsible in any way for such use, misuse, interpretation, misinterpretation, understanding or misunderstanding of this material or supporting media.

Think about what you are doing. Don't get stupid about doing it.

Thank you, and good luck as you begin and/or continue your training and education.

Introduction: Still Answering That Question...

In the Introduction to Volume One of this series, I presented my paraphrase of the "CWS Question" to you. For reference, I will repeat it here:

"What you could do twenty years ago, or even ten years ago, might be interesting but does it really matter <u>now</u>? No. What you could do 'back in the day' doesn't matter. What matters is what you can do <u>right here</u>, <u>right now</u>. The trouble that you handled a decade back in the 'good old days' isn't the trouble that's coming to you now. <u>What can you do now</u>? Are you ready to throw down <u>right here and right now</u> if you need to, if you have to? <u>Are you</u>? <u>Can You</u>?"

I answered that question for that time in Volume One. But that was then, this is now, and the question remains, because that was then and this is now, and answering and getting ready to answer and being able to answer that question is an ongoing process because the question itself is an ongoing question. And ongoing questions need ongoing answers.

Besides all that, anybody that spends even a little time on the subject of the fight, even narrowed down mostly to the fight with guns, figures out quickly that there's much, <u>much</u> more to the study of the fight than can be put into one book of approximately 120 pages as Volume One is.

So here I am, back again, still (to borrow from Bruce Lee) pointing my finger at the moon. Because, like you, I have to answer the CWS Question too. Part of my answer is to try as best I can to help you answer that question as best you can, correctly.

That's what I can do now.

What can you do?

I hope, the same way I did and still do with Volume One, that you will find something here that will help you answer that question the right way, some day, when life is on the line.

Good luck.

ABOUT THE PICTURES IN THIS BOOK

All the safety rules were followed in the production of the photographs used in this book. In all cases where shooting was not involved, verified-empty weapons or replica weapons were used. Where a weapon is pointed at the camera, it is either a replica, verified empty, the camera is unattended, or a combination of those states. Where live-fire is shown, either the photographer is behind the line of fire or the camera is being operated on a timer or remotely. No one was allowed to 'break the plane' at any point of a live-fire sequence.

A message to the Four Rules Absolutists out there:

I realize that there is a minority out there that will look at some of the photos in this book and blanch in horror at the idea that I am pointing guns directly at the camera or have guns pointed at me in some of the photos. There will be mutterings, perhaps even exclamations, of "Treat all guns as if they are loaded!" and "Do not point a gun at anything you don't want to destroy!" For those who react in this way to these photos or even the thought that someone is making photos like this (it's not just me, by the way), I have a message for you:

Start thinking and stop being stupid about it.

Honestly, if I didn't think Colonel Cooper had better things to do in the afterlife, I would expect every Four Rules Absolutist to wake up one night and see his spirit standing at the foot of the bed, waving a finger and shaking his head and going, "Tsk, tsk, tsk..." in disappointment. The Colonel understood the rules he was writing out, and he understood the way you should think about them, and he expected people to use a bit of common sense about their employment. He would understand that bullets are not going to leap out of a picture of a screen, and if he had verified a weapon was empty and had others verify a weapon was empty and was keeping the weapon under his control, he would still be cautious but he would not treat it the same way he treated one that was loaded.

He had more sense than that. Perhaps you should too.

About what I wear in photos:

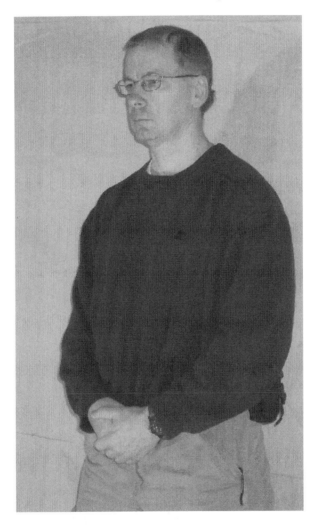

I don't have photo-specific or even range-specific clothing. There's nothing I put on specifically for photo work for this or any other book, or for video production. None of you reading this have special 'gun clothes' that you only wear when you're carrying, do you? If I'm going to do my job properly in presenting this information to you, then, I need to be showing you how it works when people like you and me are doing what they normally do.

So what you see here is pretty much what I wear every day: Undershirt (even in summer in Alabama, I have an inner shirt on under [usually] a t-shirt), shirt, pants, and boots. (I wear boots almost all the time. I have a preference for the ones with side zippers because they're faster to put on.) What you can't see is a good belt made and purchased specifically to facilitate weapon carry and the G19 in a quality Inside-the-Waistband (IWB) holster that is attached to it. And that is as it should be, don't you think?

The Maxpedition pouch you see just back of the left hip is part of my Every-Day Carry (EDC) gear just like the Gerber multi-tool that's roughly opposite it on the belt. (In a future volume in the series I will be detailing the 'Other EDC' I carry and why I carry what I do.) It carries my phone, a flashlight, and pens and pencils. I generally try to leave it uncovered on the theory that the bulge it would create under a shirt is more likely to make me the focus of a 'man with gun' call than the actual gun would.

Sometimes, when I am on the range practicing or running a class, I will tuck the outer shirt in and carry open. Normally, however, I practice and train with handguns wearing closed-front cover because that's what I wear. It seems counterproductive to me to not practice and train like I'm going to have to fight. That's why I remain puzzled by people that go to the range and do all their 'combat' shooting practice without a cover on and by trainers and instructors that do all manner of illustrations and demonstrations of defensive shooting techniques from uncovered positions or, at best, wearing vests that few others wear on a regular and consistent basis.

Don't read this as saying that everyone _has_ to run _all_ the time from under cover no matter what. I don't, and I don't expect others to. When I'm working on fundamental shooting techniques, for example, I don't worry about cover or no. Those of you just starting out, just beginning to learn, you should not try and work from under cover for a while. One you get some time behind the gun, though, once you've started working beyond the basics and training beyond the first or second class, and if you're working on your fighting techniques, then yes, I believe you should start putting the cover on. And I believe that instructors should be demonstrating things in photos and in videos from the same place as the people that are looking at those demonstrations will have to work from.

I will also move to an open-carry posture when working with a rifle most times, given that once the rifle does come out it is going to be pretty obvious that I'm armed anyway. What's one more gun in sight going to matter, then?

Also, you will see in the range photos that I am often wearing gloves. Especially when working with rifles, but also very often when working with pistols, I will put a pair of thin gloves on to reduce the incidences of minor cuts and scrapes or burns from hot barrels. (I have actually ripped the skin at the base of my right thumb open through the gloves without ripping them, so even that is no guarantee.) I don't necessarily recommend everyone do this, but I did want to explain why you see them in some or most of the range photos.

ABOUT THE CONTENT OF THIS BOOK

A lot of the material in this second volume of the series has been collected from one of four sources: Articles written for Concealed Carry Magazine, a publication produced by the United States Concealed Carry Association; articles written for a weekly newsletter that USCCA produces and publishes on the Internet; articles written for Warrior Talk News, a blog and newsletter produced and published by Suarez International; and from postings on various Internet forums where I have been or currently am active. There is more new/previously unpublished material in this volume than before, and I expect that trend to continue as more editions are published. Pictures have been added to help expand on some concepts, and things organized to follow and complement each other to create a whole that I believe will be much more useful to you than if you went through (assuming you could find everything) all of the material separately as it was originally published.

In addition, material expanding on and/or related to the work here will be placed on my company website (www.inshadowinlight.com) on an ongoing basis. Such additional work will continue as subsequent volumes are published. (Fair warning: I'm well behind in that part of the book support work at this time.)

Finally, a legal note. I retain all required rights and/or have permission to publish all material and supporting material included here.

Now let's get back to the good stuff.

PART ONE: MIND, BODY, SPIRIT

About Being Aware

I've said it other places, I'll say it here now: NOBODY stays in Condition 1 or Condition Yellow or whatever they call it (for some reason I just am not fond of the Color Codes any more) all the time. NOBODY can or does stay alert every moment of every day of every year. Not you, not me, not the most highly experienced and best-trained operator in the history of the universe. NOBODY.

I've said that before. The rest, I haven't said until now:

If you say you are always alert (and not joking when you say it), you are lying.

If you think you can always be alert (every time, all the time, every place, any place, under any condition, under all conditions), you are operationally stupid or operationally foolish or both.

If you don't base some of your plans and preparations around the idea that you will be caught off-guard and unawares, then you are being operationally stupid (this is different from being generally stupid) and you may die.

That's not an opinion, that's reality. Argue with reality if you want, but don't expect me to support you in that argument.

We are all too human to be like this all of the time.

The key here is **constantly**. You can't do it **constantly**. No one can. Not everywhere, not under all conditions, not under all circumstances, not ongoing and not all the time. Ladies and Gentlemen, I know men and women who have lived and worked and fought in places and environments where either everyone around them was trying to <u>kill</u> them or where just some of them were but they could not be sure at times of who was and was not (trying to kill them).

Some times, some places, some days, you <u>will</u> be more like this.

They <u>all</u> say that even then they are unable to maintain the level of awareness they need at all times. If none of <u>them</u> can do it, Ladies and Gentlemen, none of <u>us</u> can.

Stop trying to fool everybody else about it, then. At the least, don't try and fool yourself, and don't believe anyone that tells you that you can do what others with far more time at both ends of the gun than either of us put together have cannot do. Otherwise, you may be caught without a backup plan and unable to adjust in time, and you may die.

I would rather not have that happen, because I assume that if you are reading this you are a good guy. And I would rather have good guys live and not die.

Let's talk about some things that will help you do that now.

Train Now, Not Later. Here's Why:

There are two reasons to consider taking training soon after you've obtained what I will call the 'basic' level of hardware—a rifle and a pistol and some ammunition to run them with. One is to learn to fight with what you've got. I have written about what I see as the difference between knowing how to shoot and knowing how to fight. It can be a frightening distance when the robber is facing you with his shirt raised and his hand on the pistol in his waistband or when two men are about to break the front door of your house down at 10:30pm. Force Science Institute studies show that criminals practice and plan and study what they do. They have a plan before they go in. You should too. Training can give you that. Training can teach you to <u>fight</u> with guns, not just shoot them. **Training can give you a big head start on keeping yourself and your family alive.**

That is the single most important reason you should seek training sooner instead of later. Your life. The lives of your family. Above all other things, <u>that</u> is why you should train.

Training can also give you the ability to fight with whatever you have or can get. A favorite example of this concept is my friend who lives far north of me. He has, I believe, three rifles, and he regularly practices with them. So far as I know, he is a better shot than I am with those rifles. Where I believe I have a solid lead on him, though, is at ranges under 50 yards and where the fight would be fluid, and more specifically where the fight might be inside of a building—CQB, Close Quarters Combat. I've practiced it and gotten guidance from others about it and he hasn't. To go with the 'geek' theme, I have installed some software for CQB and he hasn't. The difference is enough that I'm confident thinking that I could pick up any of his rifles and have a better chance of winning a room-to-room fight than he would with his own rifles. That's because something in my head can say 'been there, done that' and the only thing I have to adjust for is the difference in the way the rifle operates—where the buttons and levers, so to speak, are and how they work—and in the length and weight of his rifles compared to mine. I would not be as fast and fluid with his rifles as I would with mine, but I would be faster and more fluid with his rifles than _he_ would with his rifles in close quarters, because I have some 'CQB software' installed, and he does not.

Training and practice is the difference between us, not the hardware. Open field, 50-100+ yards, he can do better. He has better software for that. He could probably pick up my rifles and do better at long range than I could with my rifles. I wouldn't be as far behind at long range as he would be at CQB because I do have some software installed, but the difference would still be significant.

The key is software—quality software, updated regularly. We need to find the software and updates to that software to work our hardware—whatever hardware we have or find—under the widest variations of circumstance.

That means training. That means study. That means practice.

And please trust me on this—you will go way, way farther, way, way faster, if you find a trainer and put in the time with them than you will on your own, no matter how many books and videos you study and how many DIY sites you have bookmarked in your web browser. You can get good, don't get me wrong. You can get pretty good indeed, on your own and by yourself. But the quality and capabilities you get from even a short time under the eye of someone experienced in both what they do and how to teach it to others is simply a wonder to behold.

So, yes, get the hardware. You have to have something before you can do anything with it. But after that, answer this question for me:

What have you done for your software lately?

Whether it's straight-up review of fundamentals with the pistol or move-and-shoot with a rifle, practice to reinforce the training. You can't let the classwork be all there is to it.

What Are You Looking For?

Training...the right kind of training, that is...can help you not only efficiently and effectively maintain awareness over longer periods of time and a wider range of conditions than you can now, but it can also give you ways to catch up and get back ahead when your awareness has faded and you get caught behind. And good training is easier to find, at least in the US, now than perhaps at any time since the first gunfight-oriented training for civilians was ever set up. There are more resources for the counter-offensive fighter at this time than there ever have been, period, end: More schools, more instructors, more books, more magazines, more videos, and more production of more of all of that, than at any period in history. It's a gold mine of information.

And like in a real gold mine, it can be difficult to find the richest veins and most valuable nuggets of information in and among the less-usable ore inside the mountain. You will have to sift and sort and process what is dug out before you get to grasp the piece of knowledge that <u>you</u> need to increase <u>your</u> value as a defender to yourself and to your loved ones.

I believe the key in considering what you spend money and time on lies in this idea:

There are sub-goals, and there is THE Goal.

Don't get them confused. Sub-goals, smaller goals, involve specifics: Learning basic gun-handling or how best to use long-guns defensively, point-shooting techniques or about fighting with a gun at very close range—things like that. We sometimes confuse these small 'g' goals with THE Goal that everybody from fishermen to full-contact fighters, golfers to gunfighters look to achieve whether they're taking a class, reading a book, or watching a DVD on their subject of interest.

So—what is the big 'G' Goal that is so fundamental that we don't think about it enough?

THE Goal is to be better at the end than you were at the beginning.

Simple as that. And as easy to miss. Bringing it back into consciousness, however, can be key to your ability to choose instruction that works for you.

How is that?

It changes the kind of competency you need from an instructor. High-level performance, past or present, is not as important to you as their ability to raise *your* performance. Tons of experience won't matter unless *they can take their experience and pass it on to you in a way that makes you better* once they've done it. That's what matters.

Ever heard this: "Those that can't do, teach."?

Let me offer a more relevant statement: *"Those that can't teach should go back to doing because they are useless to you trying to teach."*

Obviously, the instructor has to know and be able to do what they're teaching. It would be stupid to think that having the skill is not necessary to passing it on. In fact, an instructor really needs to be able to do more than he or she teaches, and to be able to teach things they aren't good at, if they are going to do the best for their students. Instructors who are 'cookie-cutters' should remain limited to organizations that need assembly-line processes and not allowed to propagate in the civilian market.

But they don't have to be world-class-A-level-gold-medal-winners to be good instructors. *Reality is, they don't even have to be as good at some things as you are going in to be able to make you better than you are going out.*

Don't believe me? Consider athletes. Professional and high-level amateur athletes, and those who wish to rise to those levels, seek out and pay lots of money to men and women who they could outperform on their very worst days even if those coaches were in their primes. Why? Not because these instructors and coaches are better at the chosen sports or activity. They seek them out and pay them all that money *because they can make the athlete better than they were before they started training with them.*

If these athletes, whose careers and income depend on their consistent ability to perform at high levels, seek out those who can <u>teach</u> better than they can <u>do</u>, shouldn't <u>you</u>, whose life and whose family's lives depends on your ability to perform on demand, do the same thing? If anything, isn't it <u>more</u> important that you improve your ability to defend yourself than it is for them to improve their performance at their chosen sport?

Keeping The Goal in mind helps you ask the right questions and filter the answers better.

You want to get better, maybe in general, maybe somewhere specific. Tailor your questions to students and, if you get a chance, to the instructor, accordingly. Look at any material, books, magazine articles, videos short or long with an eye toward determining how well that candidate for your time and training dollars can help you understand what you need to know to get better. Look for communication skills, adaptability and flexibility, and evidence that the instructor knows of more than one way to answer a question or provide a solution to you. Reduce the emphasis on their personal capability in techniques or tactics, and put more emphasis on their ability to teach and communicate and pass techniques and tactics to others so that they can do them better. Don't worry much if it looks like you have a higher skill level than the instructor you're evaluating; worry instead about whether that instructor is able to make you better at what you want to do, specifically or in general.

It's a harder thing to judge and quantify, but it is more important than probably any other criteria that you can assign a value to.

Keeping The Goal in mind helps you evaluate other resources.

Considering stand-alone instructional material, it can help you assess its usefulness to you. Does this book/DVD/magazine/online reference give you something you don't have that will make you better, or does it give you a better perspective or method about doing something you already know? It's a given that class experience will carry you farther than studying from a book or video presentation will, but the reality is that few of us can afford either time or expense to go to every instructor and every class we would benefit from. Even if you could, books and DVDs and other resources give us a reliable 'memory' of class experience that we can use to review and to build on the class work with.

As I said before, you can also use printed and recorded material to 'interview' instructors ahead of time. Keep in mind, though, that a video or printed presentation is one way and only shows you one channel of the exchange that will take place between you and the instructor in a class. It will not show you the flexibility and full depth of the instructor's knowledge that he or she will display in a class when they adapt to individual student's needs and capabilities. The best, perhaps the only, way to get a gauge on that ahead of time is to get feedback from students about the instructor and the school.

That given, though, any look ahead of time you can get is probably better than the realization that you've blown upwards of a few hundred dollars after you are into the second hour of the class.

One other note about DVDs and books and similar media. In almost every case, it's better if you can go to a class or get personal training of some kind. But very few of us can afford either the money or time it would take to cover all of the kinds of training we need, much less want, directly from schools and instructors. For one reason or another, sometimes that book or that DVD set will be the best we can do for now. So you need to look at it as if you were choosing an instructor or class to take, because in a sense that is exactly what you are doing in the absence of the real thing, and it is just as important, when it's the only thing you have, to make it the right thing. Keeping The Goal in mind will help you with those kinds of choices as well.

Written and recorded material is 1) Good for reinforcing and reviewing what was taught you in class, and 2) Better than trying to develop everything on your own with no help at all. It is no substitute for class time with a good instructor and should never be considered as such.

So: *Will it make you better?* That is the simple question that answers the question of what to look for when you examine your choices for training and study in the fighting disciplines. *Has it made you better?* That is the simple question that you can use to evaluate the usefulness of a course or a resource you have chosen. But the questions aren't really that simple, are they? No. But they're important, and you owe it to yourself and your loved ones to answer them as best you can. Money and time are the least of the things that might be wasted if you don't.

Good luck.

They're Not Here for the Social Violence

My first reaction was shock. Here's what I read to feel that:

*"In the case of an "in-home" invasion, where I become aware of the intrusion (and yes, I have early warning devices spaced here and there to give me warning), **my FIRST choice will be to engage the thug in armed "hand-to-hand"** (I promise I'll have the upper hand as far as hand weapons are concerned.) That way, there are no firearms used, if at all possible, **the BG gets his ASS WHOOPED**, and perhaps may even bleed to death on our carpets (don't like that idea either)—and my wife will not be in danger of a stray bullet from my "under pillow" piece— AND who will be at the nearest door-jam with her own projectile launcher (to back me up)."* [The parts that hit me hardest have been marked in bold.]

This was part of a discussion that followed a post I made in an Internet forum about my preference for the rifle or carbine over a shotgun for a home-defense weapon. (That posting, with expansion, is in Part Two of this book.) The man that wrote that is a veteran of long service (for which I thank him and everyone else who has served this country, whether in combat or not) who, I think, has seen more than I have of things I could wish no one ever has to see again. I can but guess that some of what he has seen is part of what led him to make what I believe is an INSANE decision about his response that I think has a high-percentage chance of getting him and his wife killed if they ever face the actuality of a home invasion.

My word on it, I hope I'm wrong about him, because he's a Good Guy, and I would rather see Good Guys win and live than lose and die. What I want to tell you now is why I might be right about him and why you should not plan to respond the same way to most any direct assault the way he has.

The problem, as I see it, is one of attitude. There is a disconnect of the attitude from the reality in this case, one that I think this good man is not alone in having. It's particularly insidious, this disconnect, because it's not a conscious one. It nonetheless drives his decision about this in particular, and others' decisions about meeting violence in one form or another in general, and it's not good that it does that. The disconnect I speak of is indicated in this phrase:

"...the BG gets his ASS WHOOPED..."

Ladies and Gentlemen, an 'ass whooping' is something that happens when things get out of hand at a bar or a party; an 'ass whooping' takes place between kids at school; an 'ass whooping' is something that I wish would happen more often to the bully and less often to the target of the bullying; an 'ass whooping' (only just very barely) might even be acceptable if it is administered as punishment to someone caught in the act of certain misdemeanor-level criminal activity.

An 'ass whooping', in other words, is Social Violence (as defined by, among others, Sgt. Rory Miller in his book Meditations On Violence, which I recommend you add to your reading list).

A home invasion is not.

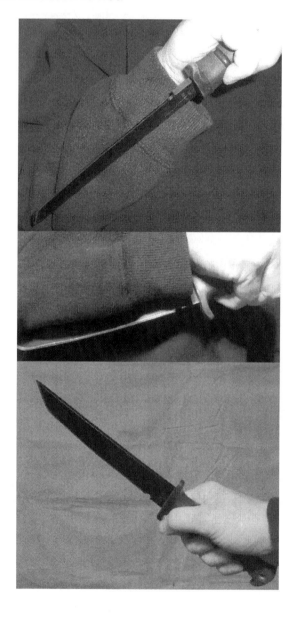

DOES THIS LOOK LIKE SOCIAL VIOLENCE TO YOU?

Your home is not being invaded because someone is trying to teach you a lesson.

Your home is not being invaded because someone is looking to set their, or your, place in the pecking order.

Your home is not being invaded because someone is trying to make a very forceful point in an argument.

The invaders of your home are not intent on committing an act of Social Violence.

Take _any_ intrusion into your home too lightly, allow righteous indignation to overtake caution, define a criminal action in the wrong way, and you could die. Your loved ones could die.

Make sure you understand that.

Get this understanding into your gut. A home invasion is an act of criminal violence that has more than once been the prelude to torture, rape, and murder.

If that's not grounds for the strongest lethal-force response you can generate in that moment, I don't know what is.

A simple study of news reports will tell you that the very best you can expect from home invaders is to be forcefully subdued while they break some of your stuff and take some more of your stuff. Even that is far beyond the 'ass whooping' response level.

And the worst that could happen?

You die. Your family dies with you. Not necessarily quickly or painlessly, either. Not necessarily before other crimes are committed against them, either. If they're really sadistic, and some have been, you will get to watch the other crimes being committed before you are killed.

And you can't know which part of that spectrum your attacker will subject you to.

Safest, therefore, to assume the worst. Because these aren't drunk guys in a bar angry because you glanced at their girlfriends; these aren't teenagers trying to establish their status in the group at your expense; these aren't bullies in the schoolyard trying to bolster their weak egos and make up for their lack of self-confidence.

These are criminals. They have come to your home, knowing that you and others are in it, to do criminal violence. They are likely to have done this before, they are likely to have planned this in advance, and they are likely to go further up the spectrum of violence the more they do this. *These are criminals.* They are there to commit criminal acts of violence, and you have no way of knowing how far they will go with you before they stop.

That's why a number of states have passed laws that state that an intruder in the home is/can be assumed to be bringing lethal force into play from the beginning, thus allowing a lethal-force response from the victim of the invasion. Legislators in those states have admitted that they don't know how far a home invader intends or is going to go, either, and they are not requiring the residents of their states to be mind-readers about it.

Are you truly psychic? If you're not, put away the idea of deliberate hand-to-hand engagement, whether with weapons in hand or not. Take the rubber bullets or baton rounds out of the shotgun. Set the birdshot aside for bird hunting, not for stopping someone that may want to kill you. Don't bet your life, the life of a spouse, the lives of your children, on the idea that racking the slide of a shotgun or showing them a pistol is going to send them away. Don't assume that the others will <u>always</u> run away if you shoot one of them. Yes, the odds are that will happen according to most reports. The odds are against people winning the lottery, too, but people still win it all the time. If you don't have to, don't take the risk of being on the wrong end of the lottery of life and death, don't risk the lives of your loved ones on what usually happens.

Because what usually happens is not what always happens. Not where real violence is involved. Not where the fight for life is involved.

No, don't play the odds, make the odds, tilt the odds in your favor, manipulate the circumstances and the rules of the most serious contest you will engage in so that they are as certain to put you on top as you can set them to be. Do everything you can do to insure that the attacker(s) are on the wrong end of every calculation.

DO EVERYTHING YOU CAN TO WIN.

Because THIS IS NOT SOCIAL VIOLENCE WE'RE TALKING ABOUT HERE. The price of you losing is not that you get your own "ass whooping". **The price of you losing this fight is DEATH.** Maybe not just your own death, either.

Get your head right on that. The price of failure is too high not to.

The Fifty-Percent Fallacy

Now here's something I hadn't seen before or since: During a private lesson for a small group that I did over three years ago at the time of this writing, the range owner stopped all activity in order to make a twenty-minute commercial presentation about his range and the courses he offered. A novel experience to me, it was, up until his final statement at the end of the commercial:

"You will only be half as good as your best day at the range!!!"

That was not novel to me by a long shot. I'd heard it before. More than once. From different people. Let's call them the "Fifty-Percenters". You've probably heard them say that yourself if you've spent much time in the gun-world.

I'm not at all sure I agree with them no matter how many times I hear it or who says it, **BUT**: *They may have a point.* Because some people won't do as well when life is threatened as they will on the range. Then again, there are those that will respond as they have trained to do so. There are even a few who do better in the fight than they do on the line in practice. And I think there's a reason for the difference in those responses other than it being part of the nature of some particular human. That difference, furthermore, is something that you can do something about.

What is the difference? Because if you know that, you know what you need to do to make a liar the Fifty-Percenters. You want to do that, right? You would rather be as good as you can be, and win and live, rather than only half as good, with its increased risk of loss and death. Half as good is an unacceptable difference when you're talking about a fight for life.

So what factors reduce your chances of dying and increase your chances of living? I think there are two:

The kind and quality of the training you get is an important factor.

Notice that I did <u>not</u> say that training, period, is a factor. It is entirely possible to get quality training that will provide you consummate mastery of a skill-set that is irredeemably inadequate for the fight you are most likely to face. Practically speaking, you are unlikely to find training that is totally useless in every way to the defensive fight, though the degree of usefulness may still not be enough to meet the demands of the attack you face. Given the same tasks they are training their students to perform, some schools and some instructors and their methodologies and curriculums <u>will</u> be more equal to it than others.

Want the best odds of surviving unarmed? You seek out combatives or mixed-martial-arts instruction of some type, not the multi-hundred-year-old traditional martial arts schools. Is the last that useless? No. It has kept many good people alive and continues to do so. But combatives and MMA-derived arts are more fitted to, and have adapted better to, the current threat in your world.

Want the best odds of winning a gunfight? Seek a school and instructors that is known to keep up-to-date on the current and most likely threats and best responses to those threats, not Modern Technique, which is not truly as modern as it used to be and which has been all but frozen in its methodology and been slow about adapting to the current threat environment (if it has been adapting at all). Does Modern Technique simply not work? No. Like the traditional martial arts, it has saved many good lives and continues to do so. But it is not as flexible as other systems, and you need flexibility more than tradition when the fight is on.

What training would you prefer to take? That which makes you more likely to succeed? Or less? More likely to win? Or not? More likely to live? Or to die? Choose wisely—life may indeed depend upon it.

The other, and most important, factor is YOU, and what you do after the class is over.

Perishable skills, guys. We don't just say that to get you to take repeat classes, we say that because it's true. You simply cannot go home after the class is over and do nothing but sign up for another class in a few months and expect to be as good in those few months, or even a few weeks later in the Rite-Aid parking lot when it really matters, as you were in the last drill of the last day of the class. The precision, the speed, the overall competency that you need when life is on the line, simply will not stay with you unless you consciously and actively work to maintain it. Just like strength or cardiovascular capability diminishes if you don't exercise, life-saving gunfight skills will diminish if you don't practice them.

This requires an investment of time and effort more than anything else. What it does NOT require is a commitment to train for hours a day, to re-create the entire training class you went through each weekend, or to ignore everything and everyone in the process of devoting yourself to martial excellence.

Hey, Bud—got fifteen minutes you can spare???

Not necessarily every day, either. It's not a bad idea if you can take fifteen, or even ten minutes, each day to review just one thing, one technique, one skill, one concept that you picked up somewhere. But even just ten or fifteen or twenty minutes, two or three times a week, of dry practice or work with an Airsoft gun at home will do wonders for building and keeping necessary and useful skill-sets. Backed up by an occasional live-fire session (it doesn't have to be more than once or twice a month if it's done properly), planned, disciplined, and focused dry practice can do wonders for your competence and capability. Ask me how I know...

Chamber checks should be visual and tactile.

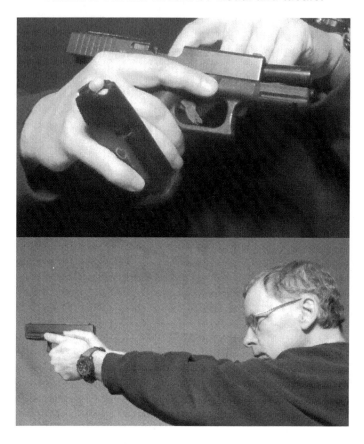

A few minutes of focused dry training (you can do more than the trigger presses I'm doing here) done periodically will greatly increase your overall skill and capability.

Training with a mirror something many of the gunfighters of legend did to hone their fighting skills. Use of photos and photo-realistic targets is also recommended in both dry and range trainng.

Dummy rounds, dummy magazines (store-bought or home built as shown here) and .22 conversion kits all have their place in the overall scheme of personal training and capability-enhancement.

And about those range visits...

Proper dry practice can both supplement range work and reduce the necessity to go to the range, which can save time and money that you can then devote to additional training. This is not to say that you don't have to do <u>any</u> live fire practice or training, only that it is not necessary and sometimes not even desirable or beneficial to make it the major component of your personal skill-maintenance program.

When you <u>do</u> go to the range, though, it should be with the same attitude you go into dry practice with. For best effect and benefit from the expenditure of time and money, a plan (not a shot-by-shot schedule, but at least a mental outline of what you are going to work on that day) and focus and concentration on what you are doing is at least helpful if not essential. You can be very flexible and you can still have great and good fun and you can do this without becoming your own personal drill sergeant. You won't get as much out of it if you <u>don't</u> enjoy it somewhere, somehow, even if you're working on something you don't like and are weak at. (Few of us are really good about bringing up weak points with joyful hearts every time, I think.) And it's not a bad idea to have a range session every so often where the goal and focus is to have some fun with the shooting drills. At some point, though, you have to eschew the idea of range time being a social occasion or 'plinking' or a 'just throwing some rounds downrange' kind of time and go to work. The alternative is to fall into the trap and risk not being as good as you are when the bullets are coming back at you.

So: You gonna make liars out of those guys or not?

It's not up to me whether they are proven right or not. You're the one that has to first get the right kind of quality training and then maintain and build on what you have learned. You're the one that has to commit to the scheduled, focused dry-practice sessions; you're the one that has to do more at the range than just shoot at something. People like me and others I will list in the Resources section of this book can help you, yes. The help is certainly there for you if you want it.

None of it will do any good if you don't put the effort in, though. That is all and entirely up to you.

So: What's it going to be? A few minutes, some thoughtful pre-planning, solid focus, disciplined effort that keeps you at your best? Or the gradual degradation of capability and perishing skills that will come if you take extended vacations between classes?

When the two guys start to separate as the one heading to your left reaches toward the felony-carry position on his waistband, do you want the Fifty-Percenters to be right—or wrong?

Your life is asking.

Answer it.

Rifle Vs. Pistol: Armament Vs. Attitude

In the aftermath of the IHOP shooting incident in Carson City, Nevada, there was much discussion on the Internet forums I monitor and participate in. There always is. We, as students of the counter-offensive fight, digest and dissect and analyze and argue (usually in the debating sense of arguing, sometimes in the usual sense) about what could and could not be done, what is or is not possible, and under what circumstances some action can or should be taken and the nature of that action.

This statement on one such forum was part of that discussion:

"I just don't like the odds of handgun vs. rifle!"

But what <u>are</u> the odds of handgun vs. rifle? Can anyone calculate that? Is there a set win-loss figure, or doesn't it really vary with the circumstance?

Does the possession of a rifle automatically trump all other circumstances?

If the man with the rifle is in the same room with you, do you say to yourself "He's got a rifle, I have no chance?"

If the man with the rifle is fumbling with it and apparently or obviously having some problems (several shooting incidents have included this interesting and potentially useful tidbit about the shooters) do you tell yourself the rifle trumps all and there is no chance? Or if he's focusing on others and not fully aware of you and what you're doing at the time? Are the odds still against you then?

If you're sixty yards away and he's shooting at your child, do you still not act because the odds are so much against you with only the pistol in your hand?

What happened to the idea that it's the person and not the weapon that matters?

So many times I've heard that. In different places, sometimes put in different words. Over and over it has been repeated, and over and over and over and over...

Is that all just a Big Lie? Or is it the truth?

Which one is it?

It varies, doesn't it? It depends, doesn't it? Sometimes, reality is that the rifle WILL trump the pistol.

Look at the reports of active shooter incidents, though. In most of them I've seen, and seen discussed, there was always a place and a time where the handgun could win it, IF the person holding that handgun had the will, the faith in themselves, and the ability to do what had to be done at that moment.

Don't you want to be able to be that person if you have to? Don't you want it to be able to make the difference if you have to?

First, believe that you can. That's the first and most important step. Fact is, many, perhaps most of you that read this already have what it takes to take on a shooter with a rifle and win. Unless you believe you do, however, you won't be able to.

So first, understand that <u>you can</u>. <u>YOU CAN</u>.

If they are shooting at <u>you</u>, how close do they have to be before you return fire? Does that depend more on the weapon, or on the person with the weapon?

From there, <u>you continue to develop yourself as a weapon</u>. Make that handgun of yours part of an integrated weapons system, not a weapon separate unto itself and separate from you. You think and you study, you train and you practice, and you get better and better and <u>you become the weapon</u>.

Once you've done that, it is only a matter of your decision as to whether and when you will act, no consideration of those illusive and illusory odds necessary.

Start with the mind, and end with the mind.

That's where it always seems to go in the end, doesn't it? The gun, your gun and their gun, in the middle is important, yes, a factor, yes, something to be considered, yes. But before, and after, that, you have to decide.

So you tell me: What are the odds for you now?

DECIDE.

When You Are All Armed—What Then?

It's a simple enough situation that we've seen discussed, and that we've discussed, over and over again. You're somewhere with your family or friends, and something happens that creates a threat to life. It's a situation where legally and morally you are more than justified in drawing your weapon and even opening fire. Over and over again I've seen the variations of that circumstance discussed, and the variations of those variations—

Except for the one where more than one of you are armed and you all know who has guns in the group.

Think about it. You may all be trained. You may all be very good shots. You may all have gone through numerous and varied scenarios involving various mixes of bad guys and innocents. You may have 'gamed', mentally or physically, circumstances where you were protecting family or friends or just other innocents close to you.

But have you ever gamed a pick-up team?

I haven't.

Consider, then. You are with family or friends who you know are armed, and they know you are. You have done some shooting and perhaps some competition together. Some but not all have taken some training beyond that.

There is a mix of backgrounds, a mix of skills, a mix of experience, a mix of capability and confidence.

The shooting starts. What do you do?

My suggestion is: START TALKING.

What are the three things you're told to do when the action starts? Shoot. Move. Communicate. (Not necessarily in that order.) What they usually say is, you should be doing at least one of those three things until the situation is resolved. I submit to you that, if you want to end a multiple-friendly-gun situation in the best possible way (Which I define as Good Guys Win, Bad Guys Lose.), then likely you will need to be doing at least two of the three if not all three beginning no later than the instant you decide that guns must come out.

Why? To make sure that everyone is covered. To make sure that no Bad Guys are left free to hurt anyone. To make sure that nobody shoots someone that shouldn't be shot. To make sure that everything is covered to the best possible effect. Because you can't assume that the shooters with you will all shoot at different things than you're shooting at. So that they know where you're going, what you're doing, who and where you're shooting, so that they in turn will not shoot you or be shot by you. To make sure that you and your friends and family get out alive and in good condition.

To help you to live and not die. Simple as that.

Okay, you say, I get why. Now tell me how and what. What do I say? How do I say it?

The idea of multiple, armed friendlies came to me when I was watching an episode of the Tactical Impact TV show that used to be on the Outdoor Channel. The hosts of the show were combat veterans with either reconnaissance or special operations backgrounds, and one had law enforcement experience as well. They used scenarios throughout the show to explain and illustrate the main subject, which was usually a discussion of the evolution of personal weapons of one form or another over time. One of the things that struck me after watching them go through various demonstrations and illustrations, which they always did as a team, was the way they talked to each other as they maneuvered, sometimes in close quarters with live weapons and, in one case, guiding an unarmed VIP in an evacuation scenario. There were no code words, no arcane verbal signals, no 'milspeak' or 'LEspeak'. But it was not a constant chatter or stream of consciousness kind of communication, either. It was simple, understandable even to me, and enough to tell the other one what was going on. Most of the time, it was whoever was in the lead telling whoever was behind what they would see and what they were going to do. And it was clear and simple. "Gun!" " Threat!" "Hold up here." "I'm going left/I got left!" "Wait! I've got to clear this corner." "Ready?" "Go!"

Common words, Common gestures, short phrases. That's the key.

Where you are/ where you will go/ where you go: "I'll take the left." "Go right!" "I'm at the corner!"

What you see/ hear/ detect: "The three by the counter. One's got a gun."

Directions/ suggestions/ instructions: "Once I draw attention, start at the right one." "Move away from me when I shoot."

Status/ description: "I'm empty!" "He's down!" "One with a gun, down the hall." "It's clear!"

If you're in a situation where silence is golden, then the same kind of hand gestures, pointing, and waving you use in normal times will work as well. There is a large list of hand signals that have been published that SWAT teams use, but you don't need all of that. You just need something that friendlies and allies will understand. You've got that already. You can also close in and whisper or mouth the words silently or write a note on something.

Whatever's gonna get you home, right?

Some of what others need to know includes where you are, where you're going, what you're doing, how you're doing. And you need to know the same things about them. You all need to know some things about what the bad guys are doing. Everybody doesn't necessarily need to know everything, but usually more information is better than less in this case. But it's not going to happen by telepathy. You're going to have to talk to each other, you're going to have to signal each other. It has to be clear, it has to be understandable, and it has to be easy. So, unless you spend a lot of off-time with other members of your SWAT team, you'll have to do it plain and normal, just like the highly-trained and highly-experienced combat veterans on TV did.

Facing a gunfight is bad enough on your own, and it's natural to think about having other friendly guns around when the bad guys come as being a Good Thing. Not necessarily, though. If everybody doesn't know what everybody is doing at the time, there's a lot of room for very serious errors there, too. The more thinking you can do about that ahead of the developments, the better chance you have of making the most serious errors the ones the bad guys made by choosing you as a target.

Part Two: Ways, Means, Manners

GET THIS IN YOUR HEAD. GET IT IN YOUR HEAD GOOD. AND DON'T FORGET IT. EVER.

Understand this fundamental concept:

The weapons you carry—guns, knives, clubs, pepper spray, whatever—may, at a time and at a place <u>not</u> of your choosing, be the <u>ONLY</u> thing between you and someone that is trying to <u>KILL</u> you (or others).

THE.

<u>ONLY</u>.

THING.

Understand?

That weapon and what's in it and on it and whatever skill and training you have with it may, without warning, be placed between you and a threat to your life.

However many there are. However big and strong they are. However jacked up on drugs or adrenaline or anger or rage they are. Whatever weapons they have.

Whatever they are, whatever they have.

What you have, whatever that is, is what you will put between you and them. Between them and your family (even if your family is not with you then). Between them and your life.

Do you really understand this?

Focus on this for a moment.

The choices you make about what kind of gun, what kind of ammunition, what kind of knife, whether or not you will get training, what kind of training you will get, who you will choose to train you...all of that, all of those choices, will affect and determine the final effectiveness of that weapon that you interpose between you and your potential killer.

Therefore, consider your choices carefully, and choose wisely, as if your very life was behind those choices.

BECAUSE.

IT.

IS.

What do you want looming large in your attacker's eyes? The best you can afford? Or the cheapest you could get? The easiest one to carry? Or the most capable weapon you can conceal? What do you want to have in between a killer and those you love? Yes, you have to compromise. But do you have to compromise as much as you do now? Or are you just being cheap and lazy?

A Few Thoughts About The Knife

Unless it is specifically for fighting, go ahead and select job-related characteristics. Just keep in mind that you still may end up having to fight with it.

Smooth edge is better than serrated edge for fighting.

You don't need a very long blade to do the fight-ending damage you need a knife to do. At the same time, go as long as the law in your area allows you to go.

A slash will hurt more than a stab but is less likely to kill. A stab may not hurt as much as a slash but is more likely to be fatal. This is not a hard and fast rule. Don't make it out to be one. You should be able to come up with at least one exception very quickly. As far as I can tell, though, this seems to be the rule of thumb to apply where fighting with a knife is concerned.

Accept the fact that a fight with a knife is going to be messy. Depend on it, in fact. Get your head straight about that now, before you ever have to slash or stab someone to save your life with a knife. It is going to be messy. You will very probably get blood on you even if you don't get cut yourself. Don't let yourself be surprised by it. Surprise could get you killed. So get your head straight about this now.

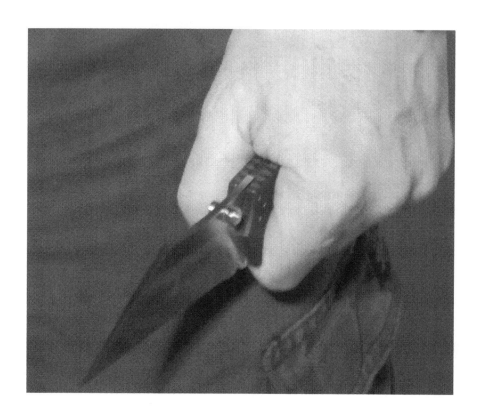

Choose a Carry Gun That You Won't Mind Losing

On one of the Internet forums I monitor, somebody once asked about good holsters for a high-dollar 1911 he had recently bought. He expressed worry about scratches and wear that would get on the gun. I'm going to hope he doesn't intend to carry the gun very much if any for defense, or that he has resources enough that he can afford to lose it if he is very much worried about it getting scratched up just from carrying it.

For anyone who doesn't have the resources to immediately replace a very expensive handgun, keep these thoughts in mind:

1) If you simply can't stand the thought of the gun hitting the ground, don't carry it. Not only that, you might not even want to take it to the range. People have killed themselves by catching a gun they lost control of and not letting it drop to the ground. If you lose control of the gun and it falls out of your hand, LET IT GO. If you simply cannot handle the idea of it getting dinged, maybe you should consider selling it.

2) If you're involved in a shooting incident, depend on the police to a) take the gun as evidence pending the results of the investigation and b) throw it into an evidence room or locker with who-knows-what, where their only concern is that it not leave that storage place without them knowing

where it went and who took it out. If you can't deal with the thought of what it would look like after it gets back to you several weeks or months later from that, get another gun for carry.

(Given that it is <u>highly</u> likely that your gun will be taken until the investigation is concluded, it is a good idea to have an identical gun locked away somewhere that you can replace it with if necessary.)

In general, if you can't deal with dings and scratches and holster wear, get another gun to carry.

Make sense? Good. Carry on.

Both solid designs, both reliable, both will do what you need. But which one are you going to cry more about when they put it in the evidence locker?

Some Things You Want to Think about When You're Deciding What to Carry

Ballistics are marginal with any handgun. We don't carry handguns because they're ballistically efficient. We carry handguns because we are frowned upon when we carry rifles and because the handgun is easier to carry and conceal and thus more likely to be at hand.

Real-world says most rounds work most of the time. Real-world says every round in every caliber will fail sometimes. I hazard a guess that none of us want to be counted in the percentage of round/caliber failures.

We beat those odds by planning on multiples. Accurate burst-fire increases the odds of winning the fight with a handgun. That given, the question is always, "What handgun and what caliber can I fire an accurate burst best with?"

Commonly-carried (and commonly-debated) ammunition in the US. Whichever caliber you choose to run, pick a gun to load them into that will minimize the weaknesses and maximize the effectiveness of that round.

Minimum burst for my purpose in these calculations is three rounds. Thus, after answering the question of can I get the burst on target with a given gun, then I want to know many bursts are in the gun/in the magazine. For example:

Most snub-nose revolvers: 1 2/3rds.

A Smith & Wesson 686 revolver: 2.

A Glock 19 (compact 9mm): 5 with normal magazine. (I say 'normal' magazine because most Glocks of a given caliber can use magazines from the larger guns in the same caliber. So, for example, a G19 could run a G17 or even a G18 magazine.)

A Glock 22 (full-size .40 S&W): 5 (There are also larger magazines available for this model.)

A Glock 30 (compact .45 S&W): 3 with normal magazine.

A Glock 21 (full-size .45 ACP): 4 with normal magazine. (There aren't larger Glock .45s, but there are 25- and 30-round magazines now available for this model.)

Smith and Wesson 686, two bursts of three. Glock 19, five bursts of three. Other characteristics may become more important, but ammunition capacity and thus the ability to sustain fire and/or engage multiple attackers is a key initial consideration.

So on and so forth. Burst-fire-shootability-wise, I won't do as well with the .38s. I'll hit better with either the 9mm or the .45. .40 S&W is in-between the .38 and the 9/.45—not as bad as the .38, but worse to my feel than 9/.45 (Too snappy in recoil impulse for me. Other people run it just fine, though. Another reason to try and fire as many different ones as you can before you commit money to a purchase.).

Next factor: FBI incident stats indicate a 50% or better (as of the time this was written) chance now that there will be more than one attacker. So, unless it's going up behind another gun, the snubbie doesn't meet the minimum requirements. The 686, good for two, but not three. And so on.

These considerations having been considered, I will start looking at characteristics like size and weight and how it feels in my hand and other aspects.

That's the factors in my minimum considerations. You might ask where specific rounds come into that. They don't much anymore. Full expansion or no expansion at all, the differences between calibers aren't enough to matter to me in a practical sense. I'm figuring to make groups of holes anyway, so the success or failure of any one given hole isn't an issue. I do prefer larger over small holes, though. So I make sure it's a good/premium round with good recommendations or history that I can hit with a burst with. And that's it for ammunition.

If you're looking at the purchase of a gun, these are at least some of the things I believe you should consider.

Having Enough (And The Right Kind Of) Gun

At the final class I ran when I was working for Suarez International, I had a student that provided me a rundown on the benefits of the .22 Magnum and specifically the NAA mini-revolver as a carry weapon when he thought he was unable or was just unwilling for some reason to run a larger gun of 9mm caliber or above. When I wondered at him about going with a least a .38 or .380 in the pocket if he was not going to go 9mm or higher, he gave me two primary reasons for running the NAA besides the fact that it is very small and light and easier to pocket than things like an LCP or a J-Frame:

1) According to him, the .22 Magnum round hit about as hard as a .380 (I hope I recall that part correctly).

2) Lots of police officers and gun-store owners (that he knew) carried and recommended them. This last fact was a key point in favor of the gun/ammo combo in his mind. If it was good enough for them, it was good enough, the reasoning seemed to go. This was the point that stuck in my mind most.

What I remember thinking at the time was that 1) everybody in those groups he mentioned was wrong and I was right in not being in favor of it, 2) I should get on with the class and not take time out for a longer debate about it, and 3) I would think about this because maybe he, and they, really do have a better point than I think they did at the time.

Well, I've been thinking about it a while, and after thinking about it, I feel good about making the following conclusion:

<u>I am still right, they are all still wrong</u>.

All of them, every one. Well meaning, perhaps well considered, I have few doubts about that. Still, they're all wrong about this. Here's why:

The smallest reason I have for saying they're wrong is concern about the ballistics of the round itself. I do believe the .22 Magnum, even the .22 Long Rifle, is better than a sharp stick, but I admit to wondering if it's better than a sharp stick when it (the round, not the stick) is fired from the NAA with its 1 1/8" or 1 5/8" barrel. I'm prepared to believe (Not that I do believe, but I am prepared to if the evidence is there.) it could be equivalent to a .380 when fired from a larger gun with a longer barrel, but most every caliber I know of suffers in performance when fired from a short-barreled gun. And I do wonder if the .22 Magnum isn't going to have the same problem in this platform. That and it's still a .22, no matter it's a Magnum and no matter what the gun it's shot from. I know they kill people, but I also hear that they don't kill them fast enough to keep them from killing somebody else before they die. Pistol rounds are marginal in general, but some are more marginal than others, and I wonder if this isn't the case with this gun/ammo combination here.

More important reasons for voting against the NAA mini-revolvers in general are:

They're very small and they're single-action. Bursts of fire are going to be practically impossible. I am a big fan of accurate burst-fire as a solution to problems that need a gunfire solution in the first place. The shootings I read or hear of and the experience of those I hear from and listen to indicate that burst-fire is better, and gunfight training should be conducted with that in mind. I don't see how anyone can put a rapid burst of rounds into an attacker with this gun from a no-warning start, especially when conditions don't allow dry hands or for you to be standing relatively still while you draw and shoot. As small as they are, I just don't see how someone would manipulate the hammer and trigger for repeat shots with any facility or with any speed under fight conditions. And speaking of bursts:

They're at best 'one-felon guns'. I have the same feeling about J-frames and some .380s and pocket-9s as well. Given a minimum of a 3-round burst (arbitrary, yes, but it's mine and I'm going to keep it), and even ignoring the problems of firing a burst from the mini-revolver to begin with, you get one, at most two, bad guys out of the gun. (Most small .380s I can think of will get you two.) Combine that with questionable ballistics and I just have to wonder why anybody thinks this is going to be the thing to have in your pocket when you leave the house. (I think I know why, but I don't think effectiveness as a weapon has anything to do with it, much as they want to think or tell you it does.) I realize a lot of attacks are stopped with one or two rounds. I also realize a lot of attacks are not. Do you want to bet your life on a single round, or a couple of rounds, doing the job? Do you, really?

**Left to Right: .22 Long Rifle (Magnum is longer and holds
more powder, thus higher muzzle velocity.), .380 ACP (also
has other names), 9mm. There are a number small, easily
concealable semi-auto pistols that fire either of the larger
rounds and that hold more of those larger rounds than the
NAA. Magnum round or no, why would you <u>not</u> want to have
the bigger bullet that you can carry more of and fire both
faster and more accurately?**

*Precision and long(er)-range shots? I don't think so with
this one.* I'm sure somebody could post a link to a
YouTube video of somebody ringing steel at 50 or 100
yards with one of these. As far as it goes, I watched
Suarez International Instructor Jon Payne get pretty boring
hitting at fifty yards with J-Frames and .380s one afternoon
in Texas. I know that J-Frames will hit reliably at 100-plus
yards in the right hands, too. But there have to be some
limits, and this seems to be one of them. The student who
gave me the rundown at the class is a contractor, I think
general construction but maybe a roofer. He's going to be
carrying the NAA in places and on structures that will
require a shot at much farther than contact range if
somebody goes nuts in his area or decides him and his
work crew is worth pulling a gun (or guns) on. I'm having
trouble believing that he (or the majority of us that aren't
remarkable enough to be on YouTube shooting 'long' with

one of the mini-revolvers) is going to be able to make the aimed shot they may need to with that gun. The guys with rifles in the mall? The shooter with the AK at the IHop? Difficult at best is an understatement with this one.

You want to bet your life on being able to hit with an NAA in .22 Magnum at 25 yards? Fifty? Do I hear 75? What about making the no-reflex shot you need on a hostage holder at ten or twenty feet? You want to bet somebody's life on that?

Perhaps a very, very good shooter could take one of these and beat someone else who is less skillful who is using a 'regular' gun. Perhaps. If the less skilled one can hit much of what they aim at, I'm still betting on that one. Skill overcomes 'strength', but I learned the hard way it only overcomes it to a point, and it's true with both bare hands and guns. And think how much stronger that very, very good shooter would be with at least a solid pocket than with that NAA mini.

Bottom line: Having 'enough gun' means more than having one of a particular caliber or one that fires a powerful round. It means having one you can fire quickly, accurately, fast, and farther than you think you might have to under as many different circumstances and in the widest possible range of conditions as possible. It means more than firepower, it means Combat Power, a totality of characteristics that make a weapon more effective than just the size of the bullet or the ease you can carry and conceal it with. To have Combat Power, you sometimes need to consider more than convenience and the fact that something is just as good on some scale as something else. You need to think about the totality of shooting to live and what you need to shoot most effectively to do that in as wide a range of circumstances as you can manage.

Sorry, but an NAA mini-revolver in .22 Magnum caliber is not enough for that. Neither are a number of guns and calibers, in my view.

Are there times and places where it should be considered?

Absolutely and without a shred of doubt in my mind. .22 LR, .22 Mag, .32, other 'minor' calibers, mini-revolvers, mini-handguns in general, all have a place and a time when they're going to be the best if not the only choice. But to carry one of those as a choice over another weapon with greater capability, even when it's only a little harder to carry that other weapon?

Remember the introduction to this section, to Part Two? No matter when, no matter where, no matter who and how many there are, what they are and how they're armed—is that NAA mini-revolver what you want to be the only thing that's between you and them? Between you and your life?

I can't see it, and I can't accept it. No matter how many police officers and gun-store owners believe it to be so. Because my life and the lives of others is worth more than the tiny bet I consider the NAA to be. If I'm going to be caught up in a high-stakes contest like a gunfight, I want to put as much on that bloody table as I can possibly manage.

Don't you?

Having Enough Gun 2: Cheap Vs. Affordable, Easy Vs. Capable

The NAA .22 LR or .22 Magnum mini-revolver as discussed in the previous chapter are 'ambush' or 'upgrade' guns. That's a gun you hide deep for when you are able to take (for example) a hostage-taker by surprise so you can either escape or get their weapon to fight back with (or similar act-or-die situation). It is not a weapon that should be deliberately chosen for EDC (Every Day Carry) for defense against unexpected criminal assault. Not when it is such a trivial matter to conceal something far more capable that will give you a far better chance of stopping that attack. Those that will tell you that the .22 Magnum is just as good as a .380 ACP may indeed be right (The small amount of research I've done indicates that .22 Magnum will penetrate as far or farther than some .380 ACP rounds do in ballistic gelatin.) but that is not the main reason they are carrying it. The main reason they are carrying it is because it is easy to carry. Ballistics equivalent to some .380s is justification, not reason.

No, I don't want to be shot with a .22 Magnum. Or a .22 LR. Or a .25 or a .32, for that matter. I don't want to get shot with any of the calibers that are routinely dismissed as inadequate for use in a counteroffensive pistol. And those who resort to that offer to another to stand downrange and take one either don't understand what is being questioned about these rounds and these calibers or they understand it well and know that they have lost the debate but are unwilling to admit it.

The point, caliber-wise, is not that any given round won't kill you. Assassins would not use .22s if they were not lethal. Lethality is not the issue when discussing weapons and ammunition choices.

 Stopping the attack as quickly as possible is.

Truth: Any round, any caliber or type of round, will work (to stop an attack) some of the time.

Truth: No round of any caliber will work (to stop an attack) all of the time.

Truth: Some rounds are proven to work (to stop an attack) more often, sometimes far more often, than others.

Here is a case where reference to some of the one-stop-shot charts running around the Internet will be useful. Find one or more of those charts. See that several of the readily-available (in the US, at least) rounds listed have 90% or better one-stop records. Note that neither .22 LR nor .22 Magnum are among those rounds.

So, no, performance is not the reason somebody carries that NAA, for all that they will tell you the ammunition in it does as well as a .380. (Not a lot of .380s in the 90th percentile listings on those charts either, by the way.) The reason is that it's easy and it's convenient.

Effectiveness? Why worry about effectiveness? Such a silly thing to bet your life on, effectiveness. Now convenience, that is something to bet your life on, yes, you bet it is...

(Just to make sure you are sure, that last sentence about convenience was sarcasm.)

There's more to this than ammunition, though. Consider these two handguns:

S&W 686, Glock 17, and equivalent ammunition loads.

A Smith and Wesson 686 and a Glock 17, and reloads that provide almost the same number of rounds. (Fully loaded, the setup shown here gives the 686 one extra.) Both are first-line handguns and great representatives of their respective classes. Either one new will most likely cost you, depending on where you buy it, between 500 and 700 dollars. (The 686 is the more expensive of the two pictured here.)

Quality-wise, neither one is superior to the other. Where pure accuracy is concerned, the 686 may be superior. Where practical accuracy is concerned (practical accuracy being defined as what most shooters training for self-defense will be able to achieve), neither one has an edge. And good shooters will shoot just as well with either one, if a single set-up shot or a series of carefully placed shots is desired with plenty of time to make them. For the average shooter seeking the most effective handgun to carry and, if necessary, use in the counteroffensive role, however, I believe the Glock 17 to be the best choice and the best investment.

Why is that? I'll have more to say about revolvers compared to semi-autos in Volume 4 of this series. Here I will focus on ammunition capacity and carry as is shown in the photo. To equal a fully-loaded G17 without a spare magazine, the 686 needs two reloads carried separate from the gun and the time required to reload it twice. The reloads are not as easy to carry or conceal (unless you use only speed strips which further increases the time needed to reload when empty), and reloading the 686 takes longer that it does to reload the G17. The G17 provides more 'fire-sustainability' and the magazine-fed pistol gets back into the fight faster if you do shoot it empty. (If you carry a spare magazine, that is. You DO carry a spare magazine? Don't you?) So for most people, the Glock 17 provides more capability for the same or lower cost.

There are, of course, handguns that cost less than a Glock—some, a lot less. (I am using Glock as a kind of mid-range of affordability standard for purposes of this discussion.) Many of them are of good to excellent quality.

But guns are also like anything else we've ever bought—excellence at low cost is very rare to find. The rule to keep in mind is that "You get what you pay for." This is just as true in the realm of firearms as it is anywhere else.

"What is your life worth?" That question comes up sometimes when there is talk of buying guns for self-defense. My answer is, "More than I can afford to pay sometimes." I think that is true of most people. Still, your life and the lives of your loved ones may be behind that gun one day. So it seems reasonable to stretch a little if you have to (for the first purchase, at least) in order to make sure you have some quality and reliability to put your lives behind. At the least, ignore any impulse to pay less, to save a few bucks, for any gun, or any gun from a manufacturer that is known more for low cost than anything else, unless you have or can get reliable information as to the quality of that weapon.

Because there are 'cheap' guns out there. A cheap gun is not what you want in your belt or in your pocket when you hear the "Hey, man..." in the drugstore parking lot, or see the man that set your inner alarm off approaching your wife as she heads into the convenience store where you stopped for gas. Inexpensive (and there is a difference between cheap and inexpensive), yes. Best possible quality you could get even though you didn't have a lot to spend on it at the time, yes. But not cheap.

There are conditions that make going for value problematical. One is where someone believes they need to get a gun now without having a lot of money available to buy one. Another is where financial hardship or low income make it unlikely that much money will be available even over time. These are valid issues that deserve consideration. There are still things you can do to overcome or at least mitigate the impact of even these circumstances. Buying used instead of buying new. If time is not an issue (if you don't believe you need something now), you can seek a used weapon, find a seller that allows lay-away or (if you can qualify) a loan that does not require interest if you pay it within a certain period (be sure you can and will pay it off in time, however, if you go that route). I have used both of those routes to acquire weapons in the past, and keep them in mind in case of possible future need. You can also do as I have done and still do and set up a "gun fund" that you put a small amount in periodically. I was pleasantly surprised at how fast five or ten dollars from each paycheck would turn into a handgun or rifle. As a last resort, a normal loan or credit card could be used by itself or combined with available funds to move you further up the quality and reliability curve. (I would, however, hold myself amiss if I did not advise you to use credit only after careful thought and to avoid it completely if at all possible.)

However much you have to spend, spend it on the best you can get. As best you can, get the best gun for the money that fits you. (Here is the paradox: You may not have to spend everything you have to get a reliable weapon of quality that fits you and your need and the role you have in mind for that gun.) *By all that is important to you, though, do not make price the primary or over-riding factor in your choice of a counteroffensive handgun.*

The life you may one day put behind that gun is worth more than that.

Combat Power

The <u>Department of Defense Dictionary of Military and Associated Terms, 12 April 2001 (As Amended Through 31 August 2005)</u> defines "combat power" as follows:

"The total means of destructive and/or disruptive force which a military unit/formation can apply against the opponent at a given time."

The U.S. Army <u>Field Manual 100-5, 1994</u>, sometimes subtitled "Fighting Future Wars," and frequently characterized as the US Army's central doctrinal statement, has this to say about combat power:

"Overwhelming combat power is the ability to focus sufficient force to ensure success and deny the enemy any chance of escape or effective retaliation. ... *Overwhelming combat power is achieved when all combat elements are violently brought to bear quickly*, giving the enemy no opportunity to respond with coordinated or effective opposition. ... Four primary elements — maneuver, firepower, protection, and leadership — combine to create combat power — the ability to fight. Their effective application and sustainment, in concert with one another, will decide the outcome of campaigns, major operations, battles, and engagements. *Leaders integrate maneuver, firepower, and protection capabilities in a variety of combinations appropriate to the situation.*" (My emphasis in italics.)

You need to think about Combat Power even if you're not a member of a military or police force. You need to think about Combat Power even though you almost certainly won't have anyone fighting beside you or at your direction, even though you will have no immediate support and none coming in before the fight is over, even though all you will have in almost every case when the fight starts is whatever you are carrying at that moment, and/or what you can find around you to fight with.

Even though you will almost certainly be fighting on your own and by yourself, you still need to think about Combat Power.

Let's break it down now:

Maneuver – It's interesting to me that this was first on the list in the Army document. I don't believe they made it first by chance. Maneuver is what places you in the best position to get the best results from your weapon(s), and maneuver is what places your attacker in the worst position to use his weapons on you. I believe there are three phases of maneuver that you should consider:

1) Pre-fight maneuvering is what you do when you think or know that something is about to happen. Before the fight starts, you attempt to position yourself so that you can make use of cover and concealment, to limit the way the opponent can come at you and attack you, to set yourself up for the best possible first shot, and to maximize your

ability to maneuver during the fight if you need or choose to.

An example of pre-fight maneuvering: Moving where you can take advantage of a 'terrain feature' (the SUV) while you watch to see if a fight is going to start. Once the fight starts you are set up to use the SUV for cover and concealment.

2) Fight maneuvering is what you do once the fight starts. It could be no more than a step and a crouch behind cover, or it could be all-out evasive footwork concurrent with the drawstroke and initial burst. It may involve changes of direction, elevation, or both, and it could be slow and quiet (evacuating a building with hostile gunmen inside, or movement from one firing position to another out of sight of your attackers) or quick and violent (explosive movement off the line of the attack). It does whatever is needed to keep you from taking hits while allowing you to get the best hits you can on the attacker(s).

3) Post-fight maneuvering is what you do after the fight you know of is over to set up as best you can in case there's another fight coming at you. The After-Action Assessment is an example of that kind of maneuvering. Moving to a

position of cover and out of the open of the shooting incident is another example.

Firepower – This is what most civilian gun-bearers focus on, and it is important. But it is not the totality of the fight. Firepower in this respect describes things such as the gun, the caliber of the gun, how well it shoots for you, how fast you can shoot it accurately, how much ammunition you carry and have available and how fast you can reload and manipulate the gun and other things related to actually shooting the gun in a fight. It is a great deal of what is studied in gun classes, and it is important to maximize firepower as much as is practical. Keep in mind, though, that having more firepower is not always enough to win the fight. How that firepower is employed is key. That's what the other aspects of Combat Power are for.

Protection – There are two aspects to protection, either of which could dominate the situation from moment to moment. Both are designed and intended to keep the attacker from doing damage to you. The first and most obvious aspect is to interpose barriers, cover or concealment or both, to keep them from knowing where you are to shoot and/or from actually hitting you when they do. Evasive maneuvering is also part of the first aspect, in that it prevents them from hitting you with their attack. The second aspect is reactive force, firepower if you will, enhanced by maneuver and brought to bear on the attacker that either shuts them down outright or makes them decide to halt their attack. If they're not attacking, you're not getting hit. That's protecting yourself any way you look at it.

Leadership – For the lone fighter, which most of us will end up being and for which we prepare to be, leadership is provided by a number of factors including the training you've had up to the moment the fight starts, past experience, and the right mindset. The things you've done before are what will lead you to maneuver correctly, bring the maximum firepower to bear, and do all that from the most protected position you can manage at the moment the guns and knives come out and at you. What you've done before to prepare yourself for this, for better or worse, is what will get you through the present troubles. It is more than prudent, therefore, to prepare yourself by considered and careful study of all aspects of the fight and to seek guidance from the finest teachers you can find. Confidence in your leadership to get you through will be essential to survival and victory. Make sure you get it now, before you need it.

That's the breakdown.

Firepower is attractive. We all ooooh and aaaah over the latest or biggest or most elegant weaponry. We debate the pros and cons of caliber and ammunition, of triggers and grips, of optics, of accessories and their good or bad characteristics, endlessly. Maneuver is impressive. We marvel when the concept of 'Getting Off The X' is first explained to us, we grasp its usefulness quickly and we apply ourselves carefully to our practice of it. We consider position, concealment, cover, pre-fight placement, and methods and ways of protecting ourselves as part of our preparation for the fight most of us aren't looking for and don't really want.

Too often, I fear, these things are considered in isolation. Not just because they have to be sometimes to be properly examined, studied, and improved upon, but because we don't think of the full and true connection between them, and we don't always appreciate how each aspect affects upon the other, how one enhances (or reduces, if we do it wrong) the other, how the sum is so much more than the whole of the parts, especially where the Fight is concerned.

We should. We must, if we want to have the best chance of being the one still standing when the shooting stops.

<u>Combat Power</u>. Seek it. Get it. Build it. Ignore the whole in favor of the part at your peril. Because the part you depend on may not be the one you need when your life is on the line.

Misfires In The Caliber Wars

Guns are nearly useless without bullets. (I would say totally useless, but you can at least hit someone with an empty gun.) And as there are different kinds of guns, there are different kinds of bullets. (I realize the accurate term is either 'cartridge' or 'round', but since you know what I'm talking about anyway, please just bear with me.) There are different sizes of bullets, different weights of bullets, different dimensions (within certain limits) of bullets, and different designs of bullets. And though the different bullets do much the same things when we use them to stop an attacker from killing us, the different bullets, because of their varying characteristics, don't always do those same things the same way or to the same degree.

Because of that, we have the Caliber Wars.

Actually, they should probably be called Bullet Wars, because it is not just the caliber (the diameter of the bullet, measured in either tenths and hundredths of an inch or in millimeters) that is argued about, it is the weight of the bullet (measured in grains) and the velocity (usually expressed in feet-per-second, fps, but sometimes in meters-per-second, mps) as well. But since everyone usually knows what is being referred to when I say 'Caliber Wars', I will use that term here.

Since I have become aware of the Caliber Wars, and especially in the time since I became a participant, whether willing or not, in the conflict, I have seen very few instances where the debate was carried on as a debate without it becoming an argument or even the verbal equivalent of a barroom brawl. Very recently, I have come to the conclusion that there are certain common elements, things that are brought up over and over again, that I now believe aren't being looked at, aren't being interpreted, and aren't being used in a way that helps anyone—whether knowledgeable or not, experienced or not—get the best use out of even the very good information that can be pulled out of these fights.

Here are some of the elements that I have come to believe are being misinterpreted:

1. I think we often focus too narrowly on the effects of a single shot.

So much is made of 'one-shot-stop' listings, so much attention is given to the wound tracks of single rounds fired into ballistic gelatin, all the autopsy photos and X-rays that look at one round and its path in a body. It's so hard not to make it the be-all and end-all of the comparisons, especially so with ones derived from actual shooting incidents. Besides, you have to start some place with evaluations. And how are you going to even begin to quantify and categorize the result of more than one hit? Damage done is cumulative, but not exactly additive, and the human body is not homogenous. Two rounds impacting close together do not double the damage done automatically; one round that hits a bone will do different kinds and levels of damage than another round that goes only to soft tissue. Single shots are easier to categorize, to set up in tables, to put into order—how can we not do that?

The danger is not that we do this; the danger is that we might, can, do, take the clinical and the statistical and make it the reality. The danger is that we start arguing about the numbers and not about the actual, hard-to-really-figure-out-sometimes, efficacy of caliber X or of bullet Y. The danger is that we might lose perspective as we narrow the focus.

Is there a reality that can be taken away from these lists of numbers? What is a usable perspective to take about single-shot effects? I think there are two:

A) Single-shot-results provide us some hope and encouragement by showing us that, as long as you're using a .38/9mm-caliber weapon or something bigger, most rounds will work most of the time (as in, above 50% and often well above that).

B) Single-shot-results also provide us a caution as well, one which we would do well indeed to take to heart: NOTHING. WORKS. EVERY. TIME. Not heavy, not light, not fast, not slow, not large, not small. Nothing, no bullet, no shape, no design, no...thing works 100% of the time. We must never assume that anything will, and adjust our training and practice accordingly.

2. *I think we 'cherry-pick' too much.*

I see this happen more to bolster negative points than to strengthen positive points. We've all seen it: Subject X was hit Y times with Z bullet without being stopped. It happens with larger 'sample populations' as well. Has anyone who reads this not at some time read a report lamenting the inadequacy of the rifle and pistol ammunition our military is provided with? The problems with one kind of bullet in one caliber turn into failures of every kind of bullet in that caliber.

But what can we do? We need the examples to make the point sometimes. I'm not sure that we can conduct a decent debate, especially one that's not going to turn into an argument, without them. What can we do?

We must make every possible effort to not take the example as the rule. We must avoid at all costs turning the specific into the general. We must not, as sometimes happens with the one-shot listings, focus so much on the tree that we don't see the forest. That is a simple concept that can be surprisingly difficult to do every time, but there may be a couple of things you can do to help you avoid narrowing your focus too much.

One idea is to spend a little time being your own Devil's Advocate. Debate teams and lawyers do this, assigning someone to research and present the opposing viewpoint. You don't have to make a major case out of opposing yourself, but finding a couple of examples that counter your own favorite examples or your viewpoint in general might help you keep the broader perspective with less effort. If you're on the opposing side of the example, remind yourself that it is indeed a single example, usually chosen to reinforce a single or limited-range statement. In general, remind yourselves to avoid investing emotion in the argument and place a higher priority on looking at larger concepts and broader principles instead of on specific incidents and examples.

It's not a perfect solution, but it may help us stay friendly when the round is over.

3. I think we sometimes forget that other things don't act and respond like human beings when they are shot.

Wood. Steel plates. Bowling pins. Phone books. Water. Clay. Even ballistic gelatin and animals. "I shot A with B and C; B did D, but C did not; so B's going to work better if I ever have to shoot a human with it.

Maybe it actually will. Maybe it actually won't. Are you willing to bet your life on it? If a bullet doesn't have a lot of history behind it—a record of success in actual shooting incidents—how can you tell what it will do when you shoot someone with it?

Humans are built like other animals. Our bones and organs are not in the same places and/or arranged the same in relation to each other as are the animals we hunt. We're not kept at a specific temperature and calibrated like ballistic gelatin is. We're not hard all the way through like wood or steel. All of these things affect us and our reaction to being shot and make us different from anything we usually reference when we talk about what happens when we are shot. Sometimes we forget that.

Am I saying that even ballistic gelatin, the current standard for testing, evaluation, and comparison, is useless? No.

What ballistic gelatin does is a) give us a reasonable idea of what a given bullet or bullet design will do when it hits soft tissue, and b) provide a standard for comparing the new and untried with the old and proven.

Say we've got Bullet R, a new design we're testing, which is the same caliber and weight as Bullet S, a round that's been on the market for some time. If I run a few rounds of each through calibrated ballistic gelatin and compare the preserved wound channels and examine the recovered bullets, I should be able to get a reasonable idea about whether Bullet R will work in practice in the same or near-the-same way as Bullet S. I can also read the reports and look at photos done by those who have run those test already and consider their results and any recommendations they make when I'm choosing what box of bullets to buy next time.

It is not a perfect system, but it appears at this time to be the one most likely to help us get home after the fight is over. It doesn't work nearly as well, however, if we don't remember that the only thing that acts like a human being when struck by a bullet is... a human being. And even human beings aren't as consistent as we need them to be when we're fighting them.

4. I think we sometimes project our 'local' experience outward and on to others.

By local experience, I mean either something we have experienced directly or something that we have seen others experience, and also something that has been related to us by someone close to us whom we trust to be accurate about the experience. I see this more often where gun choices are discussed than where bullets are discussed—"I can shoot this pistol very well and comfortably" or "I can shoot X caliber without discomfort". Then we, without realizing it, project our comfort or competence out to everyone else and wonder why they're having any trouble with it. In the case of ammunition performance, we experience a failure or success of performance or see a failure or success of performance somewhere in our group or team or department, and we project that to not just that particular brand or model of ammunition but to every kind and type of ammunition in its class or caliber. It didn't work this time; it worked great in that case; this particular kind of ammunition has not worked consistently; so now, nothing like it works or will ever work for anybody, or it will have great and good success for everybody. The specific becomes the general, the event becomes the anecdotal, and the fight goes on.

This doesn't happen very often, but it does happen, and we need to keep it in mind and guard against its spread. When the failure or the success happens to us, with something we're using, it can be especially difficult not to project beyond the specific. I don't have any advice on how to avoid it. All I can ask is that we be careful about doing it if we can.

So there it is: Some of the ways that good debates can turn into bad arguments. This in no way is a plea not to use these elements in your discussions. I don't really see how you can avoid doing so, if you're going to have the best and broadest kind of information you need to make your point and to understand the points others make. I do think we should avoid getting overly focused on any of these elements, or else we will risk missing the broader and more useful picture. We might also risk making adversaries instead of friends, too.

Everybody ready, then? Okay, touch gloves and return to your corners. Keep it clean, now. Wait for the sound of the...shot?...and come out fighting...

The Real World Vs. The Range: An Example

So, I go into my favorite pawn shop to pick up an FFL transfer one Saturday morning. Right behind me, in come five guys with the suspicious kind of look and feel to them that has both me and the employees pegging a bit.

The counter I'm at filling out forms is in the approximate center of the store. A big step right behind me is a dead-end gap between a jewelry case and a pegboard wall with tools and tool cases on both sides; that's if I turn and face the front of the store. I could go into that isle, over the jewelry case, and be out the front door.

Facing the door from where I am, the right side has the paycheck loan counter at one end and some other merchandise. The left side has the area where they keep the good jewelry and the gun section, which is large. Distances either way...hmmmm...call it 25-30 feet/7-10 yards easy.

So, I'm at the counter in the middle, keeping a sliding watch on the five guys that have now split to completely opposite ends of the store. Two of them are working on buying a gun on my left, three of them are over checking out merchandise on my right (facing the front of the store). I would have to take two steps right and go about ten, maybe fifteen feet to hit the front entrance and be out of the store, or there is a gap in the counter two steps over where I could go behind the counter and out through the back where the merchandise is stored.

So there I am getting the transfer taken care of and examining the possibilities. Couldn't detect any weapons on anybody, but I still processed the possibilities and what-ifs because this group didn't register high on the 'upstanding citizens' rating. If both sub-groups presented I could try and sprint out the front door (a big side-step and straight-on about ten feet would have done it), go over the counter I was working at and try going out the back of the store (or providing another gun to the employees if they chose to fight), drop into the dead-end isle for concealment and cover, or be stupid and try and engage from where I was standing, in the open and with not less than a 160-degree traverse between targets on either side. Go to the dead-end isle, I get concealment and maybe cover on one side, but I put my back to somebody.

At some point in my contemplation of all this, it occurred to me that *this isn't like any IDPA or training scenario I've ever heard of set up.*

Once again, truth beats fiction, live and in a store where I'm standing.

The 'take-away': Try and be as imaginative as you can when you what-if and visualize and set up range exercises some of the time. And be guaranteed, you'll see something on the street that's more complex, just like I did. So keep thinking and keep working on getting more dangerous.

Carbine Over Shotgun? You Bet. Here's Why.

(Note: Unless specified otherwise, when I say 'shotgun' I will be referring to the 12ga shotgun in its numerous variants as is commonly available in the US.)

I'm not a shotgun guy. Never have been. I've owned two and likely will at some time have another one. But even if I ever get another one, it will not be a primary weapon for any scenario, including home defense.

The reason I favor the carbine is simple: It offers more flexibility and covers a wider range of fight circumstances than a shotgun does.

Keep in mind that I am oriented toward the fight. I don't hunt, don't want to overmuch, not interested in what does best for hunting. I'm more inclined to study the dropping of people that want to kill me than the dropping of game that could care less what I do as long as I don't interfere with it eating and breeding. I'm not even that interested in rifles designed primarily or solely with hunting in mind except where the area of long-range precision fire might be concerned. (For the most part, though, not even there much. Lots of fight-focused guns that will reach with precision—no need for me to pull one out of its niche for that.)

Given that restriction of interest and the criteria it establishes, the shotgun can work, but the rifle rules. (Argue if you want, but don't expect me to care about your argument until you can point to an army somewhere that issues shotguns to all infantry units as their standard general-purpose shoulder arm.)

Even in the restricted space and at the restricted ranges found inside the average house, I still consider the carbine—specifically a magazine-fed semi-auto based on current military design and manufacture, preferably with a few capability-enhancing accessories—a better choice than a shotgun.

There are three main reasons for this consideration:

Length is the smallest consideration, but it can be an important one. Most shotguns, even those optimized for defensive use, end up being longer than most rifles. (I suspect this is because of the combination of minimum required barrel length and average length-of-pull [Distance from trigger to end of butt-pad or -plate.] they come out of the factory with.) It doesn't take a lot of time working inside to find out that an inch or two either way makes a real difference in what you can do and how well you can do it.

Carbine with stock compressed for CQB provides two to three inches of extra length over the shotgun. This can be vital when maneuvering in close spaces.

Magazine Capacity is a close second in importance in my considerations. A shotgun, depending on what model and type it is and possibly whether it has aftermarket parts added, will get you anywhere from 3-7 rounds in a tube-fed model and from 5-20 in some magazine-fed models. (There is the Kel-Tec KSG, a 14+1 double-tube bullpup shotgun, and one or two other similar offerings at the time of this writing, but they are not common enough for now to be a consideration.) Most modern mil-spec carbines come stock with 30-round magazines, and there are 60 and 100 round magazines available for some AR models and 75 and 100 round drums you can get for most AKs. (Note: Some of those large-capacity magazines have a less-than-stellar reputation for reliability. Others are reliable if they are not fed the wrong kind of ammunition. Some investigation is in order before paying for one 100-round magazine rather than six or more 30-round magazines.) More rounds on the gun, less need to make sure you have some way to carry extra when you're padding around in your underwear in your house in the middle of the night. More rounds on the gun, the longer you can sustain the fight without having to reload. (Yes, most of them will be over with quickly. If you want to bet your life on your not being the exception that tests that rule, go right ahead. I'd rather not.) More rounds on the gun, more bad guys you can stop and drop if you have to. (Yes, most times the rest will run. See previous parenthetical note about reliance on bad guys following averages where fights are concerned.)

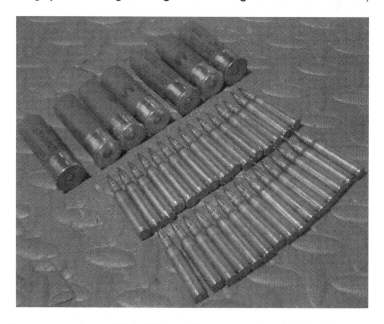

Seven rounds or thirty? Even if you need multiple rifle shots per bad guy, you still come out ahead.

It can be quite reasonably argued that the shotgun won't need as many rounds to do the job because each round hits so much harder than does the one out of the rifle. But even if I do have to throw two or three rounds out per bad guy, I still come out ahead on the bad-guys-per-magazine count. That is an important consideration for me, as is the most important consideration, that being:

Consistent precision in varied circumstances. I want it. Shotguns don't have it. Not over the range of circumstances and situations a rifle or carbine does. They can get it, in many (but still not all) cases, but not as easily or quickly as a carbine can. That is, if the circumstance changes, the shotgunner won't be able to adapt as quickly and easily to that change as the rifle shooter will. I base that belief on two things: I've patterned buckshot at home-defense ranges and I note that serious combat shotgunners practice ammunition-change drills. When the kind of shot needed changes, shotgunners change ammunition while rifle shooters adjust their aim. Who's likely to get the shot off first?

You may continue to disagree with my analysis and reasoning. I suspect that many will. As I said in the introduction to Part One of my first book, I may not like it, but as long as you've considered things and believe you have good counterarguments to back you, I can respect that disagreement and we can go on together. That's a Good Thing any way you look at it.

Oh...and whether you stay with the shotgun or not, go get some training.

Patterning The Home-Defense Shotgun

Don't think that you can get away without doing it.

(NOTE: This discussion assumes the use of buckshot (or other pre-fragmented/multiple-round ammunition) in the shotgun. If you're going to run slugs from the get-go, better to go ahead and get a rifle instead.)

Of the group of people that own long-guns for (primarily) self-defense, I believe most of them still designate a shotgun as a primary home/interior defense weapon. Out of that group, I wonder how many of them have taken the following steps to get themselves and that designated shotgun ready for use against an intruder:

1. Step off or otherwise measure the longest distance and the most likely distance inside their home that they will fire the shotgun over.

2. Take their shotgun to the range and shoot their chosen defensive ammunition at those measured ranges to determine where the shot will fall and how much, if any, it will spread around the point of impact.

If you are one of those that have not done this already, schedule a time when you will as soon as you can. I believe that everyone needs to do this at the least because it will show or reinforce two important concepts to them:

1. Buckshot will not spread as far around the point of aim as you might believe it will before you test it.

2. You have to aim a shotgun just as much as you do a rifle or pistol, especially at close range.

One of the strengths of the shotgun is its ability to get hits less-than-ideal sighting conditions at pistol ranges. The rounds of buckshot spread from the barrel and cover a wider area on and around the target to increase the chance of not just hitting, but of getting simultaneous multiple hits even under adverse circumstances such as low-light conditions. That same characteristic can also, however, become a weakness and possible liability if the shot spreads too much, leading to stray rounds going through or even outside the home with the risk of damage or injury to someone besides the attacker. There is also the risk of relying too much on the spread of shot that you don't properly aim the shotgun and so either put lots of damage on a non-vital part of the body that does not stop the attack or miss entirely and send the entire load away someplace where you did not want it to go.

To minimize those risks and play to the strength of the shotgun, you need to know where the shot is most likely to go when you shoot it from where you're most likely to shoot it and at the distance you're most likely to be shooting it at, not some arbitrary "zero" range or someone else's definition of standard distance. You need to measure it out and you need to see what the round you're shooting will do and where the shot will fall at the distance you will need to fire at. You need to pattern that gun.

Consider the fall of shot shown in the photograph below:

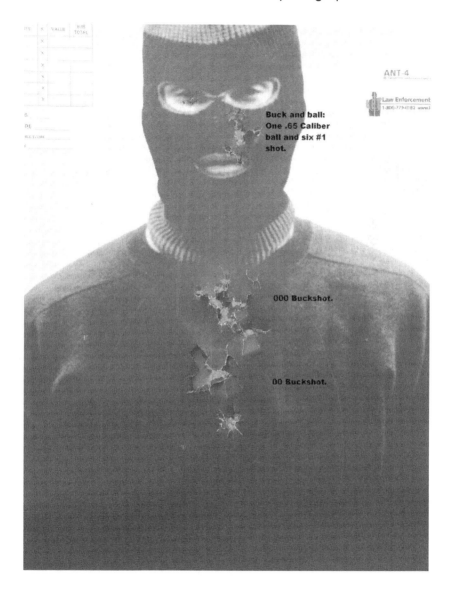

Buck and ball:
One .65 Caliber
ball and six #1
shot.

000 Buckshot.

00 Buckshot.

Each round was fired from between three and four yards,
ten to twelve feet, away. This is the longest shot I will make
inside of the house I live in currently. Note the density of

the patterns even with the 00 buckshot which provides the largest number of individual balls of the three rounds. I could cover each of those patterns with my fist, and I don't have large hands. This means that I cannot automatically fill a hallway with destruction and damage and that I cannot get sloppy about aiming just because I've got a big bore with lots of shot in it.

I believe that if you go through the process as I have in the way I suggest you do that you will find the results to be similarly instructive. You need to be sure that your ammunition is going to go where you want it, into the area where you want it, and you need to understand where it is and is not going to go when you fire that weapon at an intruder. Yes, you might be disappointed and you might decide you need to change something about the weapon, the ammunition, the way the weapon is set up, or all three.

As irritating as it may be to have to change things, isn't it far, far better to discover what you need <u>before</u> the need to shoot for real?

Measure the distance. Pattern the shotgun properly. The effort will not be wasted.

The Home Defense Shotgun: Suggestions for Configuration

Though you can fight with any long-gun as it is when it comes out of the box, it is almost always going to be advantageous to make some modifications and add some accessories. In most cases, this will greatly enhance your ability to stop a violent attack quickly and effectively even under adverse circumstances. This is as true with shotguns as it is with rifles and carbines. The type or style of weapon you chose can also either contribute to or subtract from your ability to defend yourself, your home, and your loved ones. That in mind, here are my recommendations for what to get and what to put on it when you get it:

Chose a semi-auto shotgun over a pump-fed for the home-defense role. (That's all I'm concerned with here.) Faster rate of fire and shot-to-shot recovery is the reason. You can undoubtedly fire as fast with a pump shotgun with enough practice, but are you going to put in enough practice? While I'm aware that a shotgun is about as hard-hitting as it gets in the gun world, I don't ever depend on a single shot doing the job where my life is on the line and I don't recommend that you do either. I may not fire a burst with a shotgun like I might with a rifle or pistol, but I do want to be able to follow up as quickly as possible if that becomes necessary. The semi-auto will let me do that without a lot of work.

It is true that some semi-auto shotguns are finicky about ammunition to a lesser or greater degree. If you are going to pick your self-defense ammunition from whatever's on sale that week that might be a concern. If, like me, you place more value on your life than that, you will select premium ammunition and you will test it in your shotgun to make sure it cycles the weapon reliably. And then you will stop worrying about it.

Then there is the venerable belief in the 'power of the rack' that is advanced in favor of the pump shotgun. It is true that the sound of the shotgun chambering a round could frighten off an intruder. It is also true that racking a shotgun could tell them where you are to shoot at or to flank and take from an unexpected direction. Or it could provoke them to setting up an ambush and jumping you when you come out to see if you frightened them away. Besides: If I want to make a noise like that, I can do it by working the bolt on a semi-auto. No pump mechanism needed.

If home defense is not the primary role, then by all means get a pump-gun. Otherwise, take a hard look at the several quality semi-auto offerings that are available to you.

12-gauge, 20-gauge, and .410 caliber are the commonly-available bore-size choices in the US. Of those three, 12 gauge offers the largest choice in available weapons and ammunition. The decision as to what size you get is mostly a matter of what you and anyone else that may have to fire the gun can handle. How many shot or how big a slug a given caliber shell holds is secondary to the ability for everyone that might need to shoot to be able to not only shoot it, but to fire repeatedly and as rapidly as necessary to stop the assault.

Get the shortest overall-length shotgun you can as long as you follow all relevant laws and regulations that govern that. You can, if you wish to go through the process and clear the paperwork hurdles, obtain or have modified a shotgun to be shorter than the law otherwise specifies. The advantage you gain with that will be from the added facility you can maneuver with it in tight spaces. It is an option to be considered.

Once you have chosen the type and gauge of shotgun and have it in hand, there are some things I recommend you do that will enhance its capability as a counteroffensive weapon and your ability to stop an attack with it:

Get rid of any chokes that are on it. Unless you have a very, very large house or a very, very large space in your house that you expect to have to fire the shotgun through, you not only won't need it, but you don't want it. Refer to the picture in the preceding chapter about patterning your shotgun for an example. Each of those groups can be covered with my fist and that is with no choke on the weapon. Isn't it one of the advantages of a buckshot round that it spreads? Why, then, limit that spread with a choke? You don't need it. If it has one, ditch it.

Unless it already has one, get an extension for tube-fed shotguns. You want as many rounds ready to fire as you can get. Some shotguns will require a magazine extension for that. Don't get one that goes beyond the end of the barrel, but do get as much extra as you can up to that point. You may well never need the extra, but if a time comes when you do, the need will be great. So add as much capacity as you can as soon as you can.

Consider a pistol grip if it doesn't already have one. If you have rifles with pistol grips, then definitely get one on the shotgun. This will give you consistent configuration across platforms. The more consistency you have, the quicker you can transition from one platform to another and the more practice and training on one platform will carry over to the other.

Get a sling on it. A simple two-point sling is more than sufficient. The utility of being able to sling the gun on demand to get your hands free while keeping it with you as you move around is well worth the small cost of a sling. Think carefully, however, about 'bandolier' slings that have loops for carrying extra shells in. That's going to add swinging weight to the weapon and alter the characteristics of sling-involved manipulations, maybe to your detriment. Make sure you put in some work with it before you decide to make it a permanent part of the weapon system you are building.

Put a red dot on it. We've established that you've got to aim a shotgun like you do a rifle. A red dot sight will give you the ability to aim it more precisely in a shorter time frame than stock sights, and the right red dot will give you accurate aim even when you're making an off-axis shot from an other-than-ideal firing position. It is also better in low-light than night sights.

A light is optional, but recommended. It needs to be mounted so that it can be activated with either hand or a remote switch positioned to allow that should be attached. You will not have a hand available to carry or manipulate a light otherwise. Some of you are wary, even outright against, mounting a light on a gun, because it will mean pointing the barrel where the light goes when it's on. Concerns can be dealt with and objections answered by getting knowledge of and training in the proper way and the right time(s) and circumstances where you would use that light. Properly employed, it is neither a bullet magnet nor a threat to innocents but a useful tactical option and enhancement to your fighting capability.

Other options. Other add-ons that might be useful include things like on-board ammunition carriers and foregrips vertical and not. On-board ammunition carriers can be useful especially if the shotgun is all you can pick up in a hurry. You need to consider where you mount a carrier and how much ammunition you want to carry on the gun. It will increase the weight and may throw the balance off if it's placed wrong, and could preclude the ability to mount and fire the shotgun ambidextrously. (Don't discount the necessity or value of being able to run the gun from either shoulder.) Vertical or angled foregrips could help with manipulation of a pump shotgun and handling of a semi-auto in the same way it assists with handling and shooting rifles and are worth consideration as an add-on.

Semi-auto shotgun with some of the recommended additions: Magazine tube extension, pistol-grip stock, sling, and red dot optic and optional vertical foregrip.

A shotgun is a solid and popular choice for the primary home-defense long-arm even as it is 'out of the box'. But almost any stock gun of any type can be enhanced and its potential as a defensive weapon increased with just a little thought and investment of time and resources. Shotguns are typical in this respect. I believe that the add-ons and modifications recommended here will do much to increase your ability to defend you and yours against violent criminal assault. Consider them, and their advantages, and get what will work best for you.

And don't forget to get some training with it.

Your Natural Reactions and Training Out Of Them

In a practical sense: You can't.

'In a practical sense' meaning 'given the time and resources that most of us who carry guns have'. It is possible to condition yourself or to be conditioned by others to over-ride or ignore very nearly any autonomous or natural physiological or psychological response we make to a given stimulus. Military organizations and other groups do it all the time. There are proven methodologies and programs for doing it.

These organizations that do it have those programs and have the resources and have the time to do that. They can, and do, allow (even mandate) people to focus on the kind of training and take the necessary amount of time to learn to over-write their previous natural programming. The ability to do that is what makes good soldiers at a lower level and good Special Forces operators at a higher level.

The question is not "Can it be done?" however. The question is "Can we (that is, you and me and everyone outside of those organizations with their programs and methodologies and resources for implementing them) do that?"

We don't work for the government. We're not even on a front line somewhere, much less a full-time operator in some direct action/covert/black-ops/special forces unit. We're not either training all day or running an op all day. We are not supported in our training or our work by a government or other large organization. We work jobs, we support families, we have to pay bills and do chores and run errands. Available training time is short, resources to pay for training from others comes from what remains when the necessary things are taken care of. We dedicate time and resources to this effort, they are not dedicated for us by others. We do this because we believe it to be important to do, not because it's the job we have signed up to do.

What this all means is that we have to be a little careful about how we train, what we train to do, and what we want to train to be able to do. You want your training to make you better, not make you confused in the moment of action. You want your training to help you fight better in the parking lot under streetlight, not make you shoot better on the range on a sunny day.

Your body and your mind don't want to do this...

...as much as they want to do this.

Once the shooting starts, you are more likely to be doing
something like this...

...than something like this.

In order to maximize the effect of your personal training and to get the most out of every dollar you put into outside training, I believe you need to do two things:

1) Identify which natural responses can be modified most easily and quickly—which ones you yourself can hope to be able to alter on your own or with minimal guidance, in other words—and which ones are beyond reach in your current circumstances of time and resources. (An example is the use of specific breathing patterns to reduce or forestall panic reactions.)

2) Find the schools, the instructors, and the fighting systems that work with and not against nature and physiology and commit your money and your time and focus to that kind of training.

The flinch response, with proper training, can be turned into a defensive counter or set you up to make such a counter. Target focus can be developed so that it increases your hit probability. Breathing patterns can be trained that will increase your ability to make a precise shot and to help you concentrate on the fight. There are instructors and schools that understand how to do this, the best ways to do this, and that will teach you how to continue to develop your ability to control what you can after you have finished the class.

The startle/flinch response can be turned into preparation for defensive action.

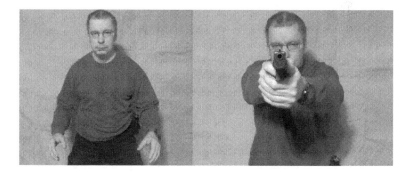

The tendency to square yourself to the perceived threat and focus on it can be used to orient a weapon or, in certain cases, as an alternative aiming technique by itself.

There are also instructors and schools that cannot or will not do this. There are some who believe, or want you to believe, that they can train you out of your base physiological reactions, that they can get someone to ignore those reactions within at most a few days of training. History has demonstrated otherwise. Long-established systems and skill-sets from a number of different martial arts including gunfighting systems have not just broken, but shattered once fists began flying, knives started stabbing and bullets started humming around the practitioners. It may take some time and effort, but it is important to identify those who go against your nature in their training and practice and avoid them. The efficiencies you will gain and the greater effectiveness you get from going to the right schools and instructors will be well worth the time it takes to identify and avoid the wrong ones.

Your time and your money are important. You want to spend them wisely. So seek out instructors that know that it is far, far better to work with Mother Nature than against her. There are more of them out there now than there used to be. Go and work with them. Give them your business. Ignore the siren call of the others lest you find yourself broken over the reefs of Reality.

Don't try to fool yourself, don't try to fight yourself, and don't listen to anyone that says they can train you to do that quickly or easily. Instead, seek those who understand and take Nature, your natural physiological reactions to threat and danger, into full account and who know how to use those reactions to help you fight better and become more dangerous to your attacker. Make Mother Nature your Ally, not your Enemy. Learn to ride that physiological response to survival and victory and to turn it into the strength you need to prevail.

Become an "all natural" fighter. Cultivate yourself as an ally in all things. You will be glad you did.

On Movement, Part One: Why Do So Many Instructors Seem To Be Teaching Movement That Is Not Fight-Relevant?

This is what I see too many instructors demonstrating and students practicing:

A sidestep.

They may draw and fire a shot or two and then sidestep. Or they may draw as they sidestep, shoot, then sidestep back to where they were. Or they may sidestep before they draw and shoot. And they always pull the gun in just as they begin to sidestep. It all looks very careful and deliberate, whether it's a single person demonstrating or a line of students in training.

Shoot, sidestep, shoot. Or, sidestep, shoot, sidestep. And don't forget to bring that gun back in when you move.

It doesn't look like evasive or combative-effective movement to me, it looks like some kind of dance:

Pull-the-gun-in-tight,

Step-to-left-or-step-to-right,

Put-your-gun-out-straight,

Take-the-shot-don't-he-si-tate,

Pull-the-gun-back-in,

Do-it-o-ver-a-gain,

DO-IN'-THE-SHOOTIN'-CLASS-SHUFFLE...

Above: Example of lateral movement while shooting as I usually see it done. Shoot, pull gun in, drop and sidestep, come up and extend, shoot. Repeat. Good if you're wearing armor (Maybe, but I prefer letting the armor become the last-ditch defense measure, not the main or only one.) or need more precision shots, but if you can help it do you really want to stop and give them a whole-body static target?

That is their recommendation and their instruction about moving and shooting.

It is not mine.

There's a few (a very few, as far as I can tell) that might, sometimes, push the envelope on this movement. Instead of a quick shuffle-step or crab-step, they will actually take a fast lunge-step or drop-step off the line, maybe, sometimes, adding one step more, while they draw.

Then they will stop. And set. And shoot.

Above: From a 'standing start', many instructors teach a single sidestep concurrent with the drawstroke, then to stop and fire your first shot(s).

Both of these options are better than standing still and expecting a scriptwriter to come through for you, but I believe there are better options that will enhance your ability to survive and win.

That is their recommendation and their instruction about moving and shooting.

It is not mine.

What bothers me even more than that, however, is the one or two that I bet I would still see if I still had those cable TV channels, the ones demonstrating a movement response of a straight back shuffle while shooting, during or after which the demonstrator will explain that "Distance is your friend." That one actually makes me a little bit nervous when I think about it now.

That is their recommendation and their instruction about moving and shooting.

It is not mine.

It is not the recommendation or the instruction of those who have made, and still make, a point of studying what tends to happen most often in real fights, either.

The reason it isn't recommended or taught by those who continue to look at what happens in an actual gunfight is that what others recommend and teach doesn't _fit_ what happens in that actual gunfight—more accurately, what happens in the most common kinds of actual gunfights they look at. They don't teach sidesteps or stopping to shoot or shuffling backwards as default gunfight solutions because they see that real people in real fights don't often, if ever, really _do_ that.

The question is why so _many_ instructors (including a few that teach supposedly 'modern' or 'progressive' or 'new' or 'updated' systems of shooting and gunfighting) demonstrate this kind of movement, apparently recommend this kind of movement, and run their students in classes through this kind of movement? If it doesn't fit the reality of most (civilian) gunfights, and they are (supposedly) teaching people to fight with guns, _why are they teaching this_?

The answers to that question that I come up with make me uncomfortable. I believe you will understand why as I relate them to you:

It's the way it's always been done. Their instructors set it up that way, they have always trained movement that way, so that's the way they do it. "It's the way we've always done it." That phrase is the bane of real progress, and in the context of the fight might just get you killed if you adhere to it.

The obvious question this idea raises is: "HAS it really ALWAYS been the way it's been done?" Keep in mind that the modern civilian-oriented training industry has not been in existence nearly as long as it seems like at times. There have not been that many generations of instructors to go back through to pin this tradition on. And if you go beyond that, to the old writings and the old stories and the older history of gunfights that we can find, you find out that they didn't actually move like that when fighting either.

Tradition is not a bad thing to have, but I do have problems with it when it might get you killed if you adhere to it. Just because your guys do something a certain way because their guys did something a certain way, that doesn't mean it's still the right way (or ever was, for that matter). Every so often, someone needs to ask the questions about the way things are done, and in asking they need to refuse to be satisfied with that particular answer until it is proven that it is <u>still</u> the <u>right</u> answer.

It's easier and more convenient for them to do it that way. Doesn't take as long to set up, doesn't take as long to make them clear about what to do, easier to monitor. Okay, I get it. It's easier for the instructor to drill me in a way I'm not likely to be acting in a gunfight. So, exactly <u>why</u> should I be <u>paying</u> <u>them</u> for <u>their</u> convenience? I'm not really clear about that.

They don't believe you, the student, can do it. Honestly, I do think some of them just don't think the average non-military non-law-enforcement student can handle 'real' training. It's not just where movement is concerned, either. Ever heard the acronym Ell-Cee-Dee? (LCD) That's Lowest Common Denominator, and that's the standard some instructors train you too. An LCD trainer either walks on to the range with a low-performance-student standard in mind, or they will adjust the class as they go to what they perceive is the lowest-level, least-capable student they have in the group. Everybody else gets to live with it because they're the instructors and they know better.

Or is that really it? Why they do that? Or is it...

...or is it that they know if they raise the standard of training that maybe the students really can (and they usually can, believe me) grasp the material and run to the limits with it? And when that happens that instructor will have to have some real <u>meat</u> of instruction for them, and that instructor might have to...Oh, the Humanity!...WORK for them! They will have to observe and adjust and pay more attention to every student and they will have to be flexible and adaptable and maybe even have to get away from the memorized list of drills and the carefully-rehearsed and well-worn (down) routine that they are so comfortable with.

What a frightening concept...to those that don't believe in what you can do and what you can be taught to do no matter who you are and where you come from.

They don't know there are other ways and better ways. Some simply don't know. They haven't looked around, haven't continued to study the art they teach, haven't opened themselves to the possibilities or paid attention to new developments and information that's been coming out. Why they haven't...I don't know. I would think that part of the job of an instructor (if they want to stay current and/or move forward in their chosen field) is to stay current and be aware of new and useful developments. If you identify anyone that doesn't appear to be doing this, that doesn't seem inclined to remain a student even as they work as teachers, I would suggest that you don't do business with them. You need the best you can get out of them, not a looped recording of what they learned up to a point in the past.

They believe that it is the best response, period. Some apparently do. One, a well-known instructor, on an instructional video I looked at recently, said it (laterally sidestepping) was the <u>best</u> way to move. No qualification, no limitation, no better places or worst places. The <u>best</u> way. Period.

He's wrong, of course. Anyone who believes like he does is. All it takes is a little thought to find places and times where the standard sidestep as he and others teach it will not only not work, but probably do more harm than good to your defensive effort. Despite such easy demonstration of the exception, though, some will, I dare say, continue to believe the blanket statement.

The fact is, there is no one <u>best</u> way to evasively move, period, no exceptions. Some ways will work better than others some times in some places, worse than others at other times and other places. The <u>best</u> way to go about the study of evasive movement is to

1) understand that there is no one-size-fits all and then to 2) find the instructors who also understand that and let them show you what the options are, the strengths and weaknesses of each option, and the times and places one is more likely to be better than others.

Photo sequence above: IDPA target behind me with tape along the centerline shows how far an attempt at a standard sidestep gets me out of the line of fire: Not completely. The attacker has only a small adjustment to make to start punching rounds into the upper chest and head. And if I'm acting without thought, the jarring interruption the wall makes to my sidestep is likely to distract me and throw my return fire off and end up getting me killed. Definitely a case where the lateral sidestep is <u>not</u> the <u>best</u> way to move.

In places like this, the pivoting turn (it can be done without taking a step as I'm doing here) moves body and head completely off the line of attack and allows for a clear drawstroke and quick return fire. Movements in this case are based mainly on Western swordfighting techniques of evasive and counterattacking movement.

Don't neglect the utility of movement along the vertical axis either (as shown in the last photo) either with or without additional lateral displacement. (This particular movement is derived from fencing's 'passata sotto'.)

Just like you should identify and give your business to those who know how to integrate point shooting and sighted shooting and avoid paying money to anyone who believes and/or teaches that one method and one method of sighting only can and must be applied to all situations, so you should also identify and give your business to those who teach the best and most applicable forms of combative movement and ignore the others who at best can only manage one or two steps of the larger and more varied dance.

Be warned, you will have to work harder in training this way than you will with the one-size-fits-all guys. You will be putting out more mental and physical effort in the beginning than if you decided to go with the flow and take what you are given like a good little trainee. Decide if you're going to work to get what you pay for now, before you start. You don't have to decide about whether you're capable of it or not. <u>You are</u>. Some instructors don't think so, but they're wrong about that. I've seen enough to know that. I've seen enough to know that you can do it. I believe in you, and I know a number of other instructors that believe in you too. So don't worry about whether you <u>can</u>, decide about whether you <u>will</u>. Then start your search.

"I don't know what to look for," you may be saying, "If what I see is not always the best option for evasive movement, what is?"

Time for Part Two.

On Movement, Part 2: Additional Options

What is fight-relevant movement?

It is movement that reduces your chances of getting hit and that increases your chances of winning the fight.

Now let's expand on that some:

What are the two main priorities in a gunfight? (Subservient to surviving and winning, that is.)

Not being hit by your attacker's gunfire.

Hitting the attacker with your own gunfire.

Of those two, what is the most important?

Not being hit.

Consider this simple matrix of outcomes:

YOU MOSTLY INTACT, THEM MOSTLY NOT. (More simply put, you alive or lightly wounded, them dead or seriously wounded.)	YOU EVADE/ESCAPE MOSTLY INTACT, THEM LEFT BEHIND MOSTLY INTACT. (Tie, Preferred Version.)
BOTH OF YOU DEAD OR SERIOUSLY WOUNDED. (Tie, Not Preferred Version)	YOU DEAD OR DYING, THEM MOSTLY INTACT. (No explanation needed.)

Don't make the mistake of thinking that this makes it a straightforward 50-50 chance of survival. This isn't a roulette wheel at a Vegas casino. This is a fight we're talking about, and what you do and what your attacker(s) do will skew the outcome for, or against you. But you can't control your attackers, you can only control yourself. Right?

Maybe. And maybe not.

You may not can <u>control</u> your attacker(s), but you can <u>influence</u> them. You can do things that mess up their original plan for the assault, you can break their momentum, you can take the initiative away from them, you can disrupt their focus, you can distract them. These things create openings of various kinds, physical, emotional, mental, and provoke them into making mistakes that you can take advantage of. What you can do can move those odds across the line toward you and away from them. What you can do can, and will, make one of the boxes bigger and easier to get to for you.

Movement—the right kind of movement, that is—is one of the things you can do to raise your chances and lower theirs. Movement is one way to influence the attacker(s) to do more what you want and less what they want to do.

Has to be the right kind of movement, though. The kind of movement that makes it harder for them to hit you and easier for you to hit them. Some things you need to think about, about that right kind of movement, include:

(One thing: No hard-and-fast rules, no guarantees involved with this. As I said before, there are times and places where Grouchos and Crabs will be the thing to be doing. And you can do everything right and still get hit and still lose. Nothing certain here, just better odds one way or the other.)

No windup. Movement has to start with as near to zero warning to the bad guy as you can manage. You will usually be starting from behind with this, and giving them a clue that you're going to move and where you're going to move is not the way to start catching up.

Explosive initiation and sudden change. The start of movement has to be not just sudden and surprising to the other side, it has to initially move or displace you very-most-quickly. If you are moving and need or decide to change your movement or movement state, that change has to be like the initiation, with little to no warning to the attacker and the quickest possible alteration of your state of movement.

Photos showing examples of dynamic evasive movement illustrating the kind of displacement that is possible. Here I am moving to my approximate 2 o'clock and 10 o'clock drawing to first shot(s) as I move. This is not a drop-step or slide-step, but an evasive take-off derived (in this case) from Southwest Asian martial arts systems that gets me from standing into a full run as the drawstroke is done.

This is not a start-stop movement. I will continue to move to the gun-man's flank at an oblique angle as I fire. He is simultaneously having to deal with the initial sudden change of position and angle, the continuously-changing position and angle, and my return fire.

This kind of movement-with-counterattack technique has a demonstrated ability to get you out of the line of the first shot(s) even in cases where the attacker has a finger on the trigger ready to go. Guaranteed to work every time that way? No. Better than trying to draw and shoot before he fires? Definitely. Better than a standard sidestep-stop-shoot? In most cases, yes, I believe so.

This is not the only way to evasively move even in this specific case. Other situations, other positions, other places will have their own 'best practices' that fit them and you better at the time. The point is not to limit yourself and not to restrict yourself, and not to let anyone else limit or restrict you. Learn and practice the full range of what you can do. It's all up to you in the end.

The displacement you need to make is not as large as you think it needs to be. Somebody that says you can't dodge a bullet is right. You can't. But you're not trying to dodge the bullet when you move. You're getting off of the line of the attacker's aim. It is not the same thing. Why? Action and reaction. You initiate the movement, you start the action. If you've managed to do it without precursor signs and you've done a good explosive start, he's surprised and reacting. You've got about .25 seconds on average to get yourself about half an inch off the line of aim.

That means moving around half of your head or body far enough to get a half-an-inch off the reaction shot, the one they start pressing the trigger on as soon as they see you move. Still, is that very far? If they're sighted on your head, you need four to seven inches of displacement. If they're sighted on your body, between a foot and a half to two and a half feet. (I'm assuming an average size range of people here. Variances do occur in both directions.) <u>That's it</u>. For the first shot, at least. Not a long lunging step, not the entire width or depth or length of your body. You don't necessarily even have to move your feet or take a full step anywhere. You can get that much by bending, twisting, dropping, or turning. It just doesn't necessarily have to be large. It does have to be definite, though, however the movement is.

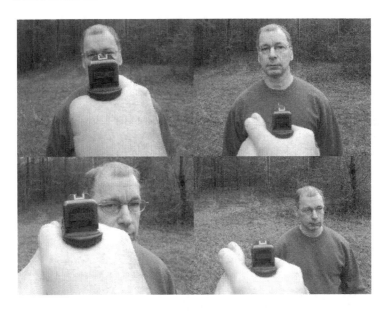

You don't have to move as much as you think to get off the line of the shot as shown here. In my case, 6 inches of head movement and a little over a foot of body movement and I'm clear. You may have to go some less or some more. The key is to understand how short and small that distance actually

is and how quickly most people can move that short distance. Solving the problem of 'how to get out of the way' is not as difficult as you might think.

Previous Pages: Examples of alternative movement patterns. I'm still moving to the 10-11 or 1-2 o'clock positions in this example, but the step and shift is different than what was shown in the earlier photo sequence. This particular movement is similar to what was done in the hallway sequence shown earlier, but on a larger scale. As in the previous example, I do not stop in either position but will continue to move and maneuver to give the attacker the hardest 'tracking' problem I can and to make my own return fire more accurate and effective. (Movement is not just evasive, it is also part of the process of fighting back effectively and successfully.) Note the level of the gun in the end photo of each movement sequence. I can begin to fire at this point with enough accuracy to make a difference in the attacker's physical state at this range. Whether I start shooting at this point or not, however, the gun will continue to move up to the eye-line.

Think "rate of change of angle" not "change of angle". We both know there's not going to be just the single shot you need to avoid. Until you can draw your own weapon and put your own fire on them, or until you make it out of sight/behind cover/both, they will keep shooting at you. They will adjust their aim, or try to, to track you as you move. You want to make that tracking problem as difficult as possible.

One way to do that is to change your angular relationship to them as quickly as possible. You want to set them up so that they are having to turn faster and faster to get their gun on you. You want them to start adjusting and keep adjusting to ever tighter turns. You want to force rapid and acute adjustments on them and do it long enough so you can start making them adjust to being hit by your return fire. If you've practiced the dynamic drawstroke and presentation from full-out movement initiation—and if you don't know what that means, check the Resource section of this book for my recommendations about getting trained to do that—you won't have to force them to adjust for very long at all.

To do that, you will likely have to close with the attacker at an acute angle. On a clock face with the attacker at twelve o'clock, you will want to think about movement to one or eleven, not more than two or ten. If you want to use the compass as a guide, if the attacker is due north, you're looking at movement north-northeast or north-northwest. Your line of movement needs to be inside of forty-five degrees of the starting line directly from you to the attacker.

Physically, this makes his rate-of-change problem harder to solve and puts you rapidly onto his flank and close enough to increase your own chances of good hits. Psychologically, it increases your chances of disturbing his thinking to the point of physical disruption. Historically, some of the most feared fighters have been those who showed no hesitation or fear about closing with the enemy. Someone that's not ready for it or accustomed to it can get unhinged in a hurry seeing someone do it. It's not a guaranteed effect, but if you get it, it will help you win.

However, as the sight of someone closing to the attack can disrupt the attacker's thinking, the idea of closing to the attack can, may, be difficult for you to think about doing and training to do. I have experienced this difficulty in my own training, and I'm willing to bet I'm not the only one that has to work through it. Your mind and your body might well prefer that you get away from the man with the gun, not go nearer to it. I think that there are times your instincts may be correct about that—there will be times when the best thing to do is to go away in some direction or other. I think that sometimes, however, the best way to avoid the incoming fire is to close at an angle such that it messes up the attacker's firing solution.

"But the guy on TV says that distance is my friend!"

Yes he does. I've heard him say it myself. The problem is that he's right...

"?!?!?!?!?!?!?"

...but not over the range he...they, actually, it's more than just that one that says that...are demonstrating. Besides that, I still think it better if you can make the attacker shift laterally as well as make yourself smaller in their eyes. So at a some point beyond the range of the typical gunfight against someone of average skill or less (A note here, ladies and gentlemen: DO NOT assume that bad guys do not know how to aim and cannot shoot well, and DO NOT assume that they do not practice with their guns.), opening distance, even if it's only straight away will reduce your chances of getting hit.

At the usual gunfight distances, though?

At the usual gunfight distances, you need better friends. You need friends like I'm describing here, and introductions to those friends by instructors who know how to make you friends with them in the most effective way.

Finally, *don't let yourself go steady-state for too long in movement.* They will adjust eventually. Hopefully, you've arranged for an end to the fight in your favor by that time, but if the encounter goes more than a few steps on your part, make that cut and change that angle and move that line again.

Some final thoughts:

There are still no guarantees. The movement concepts presented here have a proven capability to keep you from getting hit, but nothing is certain and nothing is forever.

That's why you must also study the drawstroke done simultaneously with the explosive start and shooting on the move. You must begin as soon as possible to understand how these things are done, when and why they should be done or are best to do, and when and why they are not. And you can still get everything done correctly and still get hit, or you can get the first one or two rounds to miss but not the second or third or fourth. This kind of evasive movement is a help, not a surety, and you must be able to end the fight as quickly as possible no matter how good and quick and sneaky you get about your movement.

Your ability to move this way with certainty and alacrity will be helped a great deal by your being in the best physical condition you can be in. You do not have to be young and strong and fast, you do not have to be free of aches and pains and injury to learn this, to practice it, or to make it work. I have seen men older than I am, more worn than I am, and more hurt than I am do just fine with learning and performing this kind of movement. Get as good as you can be, and in as good a condition as you can get, so that you can do this as best you can in the moment you have to do it to live. That's all I ask of you. (The next section will have some thoughts on conditioning specific to this kind of movement.)

This movement does not completely replace the steady and considered stepping patterns represented by the Groucho and the Crab. I maintain that it should supplant them in the situations you are most likely to conduct a gunfight in, but there are other situations where explosive movement will be the wrong thing to do, plain and simple. There will be conditions, situations, and environments where the need and ability to move in a way that gives you the steadiest possible shooting platform will be paramount. So don't drop this kind of work out of your training routine.

And the common theme: Training, organized training under the guidance of an instructor who knows about this kind of movement, will take you much farther and much faster than any amount of self-study with any available material in any format. If you really want to get this down and get it down correctly, get to a class. If all else fails, however, there are video resources that you can get that will help you get the idea. (Specific references will be provided in the Resources section.)

So what are you waiting for? Get moving! Just do it the right way.

Some Additional Notes On Movement

When you're on your back: Some people, when they start getting up, do a classic sit-up movement to get to sitting position. This may not be the most efficient start, as it's more likely to bring the feet/legs up to counterbalance, which threatens to put them into the line of the muzzle, it doesn't really use the strong stomach muscles, and the standard sit-up motion can hurt the lower back. To start up to the seated position, I recommend the beginning of a 'crunch'; curl the upper body as if you're trying to roll yourself forward as far as you can before continuing to the seated position. Think of moving your nose toward your toes while keeping your chin in contact with your chest as far as you can to start the curl. (Look up the abdominal crunch exercise to see what the upper body part of the movement looks like; that's what you'll do.) Way easier, less likely to bring your foot into the gun-line sympathetically as you rise.

Instead of sitting straight up, you can also roll to the opposite-gun side and start getting up from there. Examine jujitsu and judo for guidelines and options doing it this way and look at exercises such as the Turkish Get-Up for ways to condition yourself to do the movements quickly and easily.

Regardless of which method you favor, practice both, and add abdominal work to your exercise routine if you don't already have it included. Just tell everybody you're working on your Tactical Six-Pack if they ask about it.

From a position on your stomach, there are also two options. One is to do a reverse squat-thrust movement where you push up and then pull your feet underneath you to stand. Or you can roll to the opposite-weapon side and get up from there. The second way lets you get to the gun quicker, the first way should get you on your feet faster.

There's also the idea of pushing up and then supporting yourself on one hand while you access the weapon. Whether that's an idea worth going much further with than speculation, I don't know.

Conditioning for the second step: Most of the explosive evasions start with a movement that puts you to some degree into a sprinter's start or lunge position. How deep you go into that position will determine whether most of the power into the second step is generated by the thrust of the back leg or the pull of the forward leg. Either way, you need to give specific attention to conditioning the leg bicep/hamstring and the gluteus muscles. If you just focus on the big thigh muscles in the front, you risk an imbalance and failure at the very moment you need everything to function at its peak capacity. Leg exercise routines have to be balanced front and back, and you will need to incorporate stretching and range-of-motion work into the routine.

Various types of lunge exercises specifically (not just a standard forward lunge) will be very helpful to you in developing the ability to move explosively.

It will help you also to study both sports and martial arts footwork. The same techniques that move a point guard around a defender or that gets a linebacker to miss a running back can also generate a missed shot while positioning you to return fire to your best advantage. When you look at martial arts' movement, make sure you pay attention to European as well as Asian, Western as well as Eastern arts. Medieval and Renaissance fighters had systems, both empty-handed and with weapons, that were as fully developed, as complex, and as effective as any Eastern/Asian system in existence. Also, when you consider the martial arts, make sure you are looking at <u>combative</u> systems and techniques, not just sport or competition systems. The old masters on both sides of the world knew a <u>lot</u> about how to move to not just stay alive, but to win.

Remember and consider that gravity can be your friend. You can use gravity to accelerate your evasive movement and to make it easier to do. All the take-offs have some manner of weight-drop included in the movement, some more than others. It may take some time, but if you can learn to turn the vertical into help for the horizontal (It's not a new concept; look at the traditional karate lunge-punch and you'll see.), you can displace faster and more smoothly with less strain on the muscles and body structure, and you won't need as much leg strength to accelerate.

The key, I think, is to make and think of the movement as continuous even when changing planes and directions. You don't drop and step, for example, or even drop-step. You just step deep and quick. Also, try thinking in terms of curves rather than lines and angles and corners. Pick a point in your abdomen or hip area, and think of moving that point in a curve instead of in straight lines as you step out and away. If you can understand the concept and work it into your movement, you have a better chance of turning the energy from the weight drop into propulsion energy for the pull 'out of the block'.

Finally, to repeat: The right kind of training will get you farther, faster, and more efficiently and easily, than almost any amount of self-study and practice you can do. Recommendations for that training are in the Resource section of this book. Invest in them, and in training. It <u>will</u> return dividends to you if you do.

Oliver Cromwell. He talks to me sometimes.

This is what he says to me:

"I beseech you, in the bowels of Christ, think it possible you may be mistaken."

I hear this phrase in my mind sometimes, and I pay attention to it, especially where subjects, ideas, facts, concepts, and principles such as I write about in this book are concerned. Because the people I am writing this for, and the people I write to about these things in various places, are too important to me for me to be anything resembling casual about it.

That's why I research. That's why I train. That's why I learn. That's why I regularly ask questions and seek advice and knowledge from people with more experience, more understanding, broader backgrounds, and larger skill-sets than I have. That's why almost nothing you will ever read that I write or see that I record or hear that I say is only and completely my personal opinion. Nothing here, nothing in the previous books and booklet, nothing in books to follow, and nothing on video will be less than an accumulation of the experience, the knowledge, the wisdom, and the proofing of and by a number--sometimes a very large number--of those who have been there, who have done that, and who know about it.

Because I listen to Lord Cromwell when he says this to me. And I know that, while I, individually, may be mistaken about something, it is highly unlikely that all of those others I pay attention to will be. Yes, it can happen that everybody, everywhere, is wrong about something. But the odds are low; very low, in my estimation. And where Reality demands that I accept some probability of error no matter how hard I try to eliminate it, I will accept very low even while I continue to work as much as I can to make it very much lower.

So when I take a stand on something—when I adopt and promote a certain concept, viewpoint, principle, technique, tactic, whatever—I do so based on the best available information from multiple sources. Keep this in mind. Keep in mind also that I will go back and review those stances and positions I take. I will go back, and I will look at everything again, and I will ask myself if I have become mistaken about it. And if I am, I will make corrections.

Because I listen to Oliver Cromwell. It is too important a subject, this subject of the counteroffensive fight, to not listen to him about it. It is too important to me, and it is too important to you, for me not to make sure, as much as I can and as best I can, that I am not mistaken about any of this.

This is my word to you on this.

Last Word Until Next Time

I'd like to think that you could substitute this book for actual training but I'm not that egotistical or stupid. Books can help some, videos can help some, sure. If you really want to get better, if you really want to make yourself more survivable in a fight, if you really want to do the best thing you can to defend the people you care about (including you), then you need to get the right kind of training from the right kind of instructor.

So the final word is two questions:

Do you want to get better?

Then why aren't you getting training?

See you in class.

Gratitude

The Lord, the God of Abraham, of Isaac, and of Jacob, and his son Jesus the Christ, continues to be far more merciful to me than I deserve Him to be. He has allowed me to continue this series of thoughts to the point where, as He allows it, there should at least be Volumes Three Four and Five coming in the fullness of time.

I am grateful also to the Staff Instructors of Suarez International and to CEO of the Suarez International Group of Companies Gabe Suarez. I do not believe that he or they even now understand how much of what I do now comes from my observation of what they have done and what they are doing now.

There are instructors who have, since I published the 1.0 version of this book, left SI and are now instructing independently. A few of those have much influenced my development and my progression as a counter-offensive fighter. Roger Phillips and John Meade are two such. I continue to appreciate their and other's contributions to my continued development.

I am also grateful to you who are reading this book. You may wonder why. Obviously, I'm pleased that you paid me for it. More fundamentally, though, is that if there weren't people that I at least thought might read these books, I wouldn't be writing them and getting pictures made up to put in them. And the questions and comments I receive from some of you help to direct what I did here and what I will do in future volumes of the series. So you, all of you, who read these works are the fundamental driving force in their production. Thank you for keeping me busy.

CR Williams

RESOURCES

Some places that will help you travel the path.

This section is about where to get stuff. Stuff for your mind: Knowledge, skills, ways and means of thinking, help with mindset and attitude. Stuff for your hand: Guns, things for guns, other weapons, things for other weapons, things that help you use and enhance the application of the stuff you get for your mind.

Any place and anything on this list has met three criteria: 1. I use them and/or refer to them now, or I have used them or referred to them in the past (that's one criteria with two parts) and consider them Good. 2. They come recommended by the people I respect and go to for knowledge and advice. 3. I believe they will offer you some kind of help or edge that you need or can use.

Don't expect me to be unbiased or 'fair' about my recommendations. Like you, I have limited resources to allocate to training and study, and I have no intention of pointing you at anything that I don't believe is worth every dollar and every minute that either of us have to allocate to something this important.

Let's get to the list now.

Stuff For Your Mind

Training resources:

For fight training:

Suarez International:
http://www.suarezinternationalstore.com/

They will teach you how to prepare for the fight, how to conduct the fight, and how to get through the aftermath of the fight. They will teach you how to fight with more than just guns and they will teach you how to use more than just guns in the fight. They will not train you at the Lowest Common Denominator setting and they will not expect you to be stupid coming in. (Ignorant, yes, maybe, but not stupid. There is a difference between those two states that some schools and instructors don't appear to understand.) They will make you work, and they will make that work worth the effort you put into it. And you will be better at the end than you were at the beginning--at fighting, not just at shooting.

If you want to go to the gun-world equivalent of a dude ranch, if you want to be a gunfighter or an operator for a day or a weekend, there are other places to do that, and you are welcome to go to them.

But if you want to become a gunfighter or a fighter, period--if you want to learn what actual gunfighters and operators know and how to do it--go to Suarez International.

Sonny Puzikas: http://gospelofviolence.com/ and http://www.warriortalk.com/forumdisplay.php?175-Sonny-Puzikas-Training

I have not taken a class from Sonny Puzikas. I have studied and learned from his DVD productions (and will continue to) and I have read what he has written (and will continue to). He is recommended by those that I listen to for advice about such things. Everything I have seen and everything I have heard of him and his instruction boils down to this: Invest in him, and he will give you things you need to win the fight with. 'Nuff said.

AMOK!: http://amokcombatives.com/

As with Sonny P's work, I have only so far been able to study work produced by Tom Sotis and his instructors. I have not been to an AMOK! class and have not received direct training. What I have seen and what I have heard of it to date, however, tells me this: If you want to learn about fighting with and against a knife, this is a very good place to go to do it.

Fight Focused Concepts: http://www.fightfocusedconcepts.com/

Roger Phillips is an excellent instructor who remains a keen student of the fight and who continues to develop that art and science of what it takes to win the fight. There is a reason I refer to and quote him as often as I do in all my writing.

Dynamic Response Training: http://dynamicresponsetraining.com/

Don Robinson worked in an Air Force special operations unit that was classified until six months before his retirement. His unit had to provide its own personnel and site security during many deployments. What he learned from that, and what he learned from others during and since that time, he is now passing on. I recommend you pay attention when he does that.

Dr. John Meade: http://www.statdoc.com/

Ignore the suit and tie photo. What's important to you is what he's doing in the second photo on that web page (he's the one in the background overseeing the drill): Teaching non-military-non-law-enforcement personnel (people like us, in other words) how to keep ourselves and others from dying even if we otherwise win the gunfight. He does that very well, too.

Study Resources: Stuff for your mind that's not training.

http://www.onesourcetactical.com/dvds.aspx

http://www.onesourcetactical.com/books.aspx

I find some things sometimes at websites like Amazon.com or Barnes and Noble, but that's mostly older material or historical reference. (I maintain a list of Medieval and Renaissance fighting system books that I want to get at Amazon, for example.) For the up-to-date material, One Source is where I look first. They have more than just SI-produced material there.

Other Web Resources: Sites and Forums

Warrior Talk web forum:
http://www.warriortalk.com

What? Do you think I would start anywhere else? That said, this web forum is <u>not</u> for everyone. For those it does fit, it can be very useful.

gospelofviolence.com

Sonny Puzika's web site.

Warrior Talk News

The SI newsletter and blog. Yes, there will be announcements and advertising of products and courses.

There will also be articles and commentaries by SI instructors that you will find useful.

Paragon Pride web forum:
http://www.paragonpride.com/forum/

A recently (as of the time of this writing) started discussion forum with a growing list of very experienced and knowledgeable people in it, all ready to help you with questions and opinions about things you need to know.

www.guntoters.com

A small web site that is growing steadily. This one is going to be best suited to those just starting out with concealed carry and defensive use of the firearm.

www.inshadowinlight.com

My company website. I will be starting it up concurrent with the release of this book. It will begin by providing additional background about what is written here and additional information and support. Additional written and video work will be added on an ongoing basis there.

STUFF FOR YOUR HANDS

http://tsdcombatsystems.com/

The best guns and the best add-ons and accessories for those guns you can get. Period.

http://www.onesourcetactical.com/

Lots of other good stuff for your guns and for you.

http://www.cdnninvestments.com/

Pretty good source for magazines. You got pistols, you need magazines.

http://www.botach.com/

Good source of all kinds of gear for all kinds of things including guns.

What's Coming Up:

Gunfighting, and Other Thoughts about Doing Violence, Volume Three:

This will focus almost completely on the Counter-Offensive Rifle. The concentration here will be on what I call short-range/short-time situations that someone who is not law enforcement or military might have to face in and around their homes or perhaps in or close to their vehicles. It doesn't happen often, but it does happen, and I want you to be ready for it if it happens to you and yours. This will also provide a useful adjunct to more conventional rifle training.

The website will be rebuilt and then continue to be updated with new content.

Volume Four of the series is planned for release sometime in the third quarter of 2015 if not sooner.

Bare-Bones Gunfighting: Book and video covering what I believe are the essential elements of winning a reactive close-range gunfight such as seems to be the norm at least in the US.

Going Live: Bare-Bones Gunfighting is also a one-day class I will teach anywhere I can get enough people together that want to learn about it. Other specialty courses include an Introduction to Fighting In and Around Vehicles and Close-Range Gunfighting, which develops on the range some the concepts I discuss in Volume 3. Standard rifle and pistol courses are also offered. Contact me through the website or by email at crwilliams@inshadowinlight if you would like to set a class up. Have training, will travel.

If you have suggestions or ideas of material you would like to see addressed, you can contact me by email at crwilliams@inshadowinlight.com.

ABOUT THE AUTHOR

What <u>about</u> the author?

Lots of people can shoot better than I can. Lots of people can draw faster than I can. Lots of people can fight better than I can. Lots of people have more experience than I do.

Why aren't <u>they</u> writing a book like this, then?

Because for all the things they <u>can</u> do better, the one thing they <u>can't</u> do better, and the one thing that's most important to you that I <u>can</u> do better than a lot of people, is that I can teach better than they can.

I am a good student, I am a very good instructor, and I am an excellent communicator. Those are the most important things you need to know about me, because that's what makes it possible for me to do the job you need me to do here and on the range.

CR Williams

Made in the USA
San Bernardino, CA
28 May 2015